Timeless Stories of the West
Mountaineers, Miners, and Indians

Joaquin Murrieta

(Author's sketch of the Zorro-like hombre that terrorized California in the 1850s; drawn from a sketch in the Searls Historical Library, Nevada City, California.)

Timeless Stories of the West
Mountaineers, Miners, and Indians

TIMELESS STORIES OF THE WEST

Mountaineers, Miners, and Indians

Rex T. Jackson

HERITAGE BOOKS
2016

HERITAGE BOOKS
AN IMPRINT OF HERITAGE BOOKS, INC.

Books, CDs, and more—Worldwide

For our listing of thousands of titles see our website at
www.HeritageBooks.com

Published 2016 by
HERITAGE BOOKS, INC.
Publishing Division
5810 Ruatan Street
Berwyn Heights, Md. 20740

Copyright © 2016 Rex T. Jackson

Heritage Books by the author:
A Trail of Tears: The American Indian in the Civil War
James B. Eads: The Civil War Ironclads and His Mississippi
The Sultana Saga: The Titanic of the Mississippi
Monumental Tales from the Ozarks
Timeless Stories of the West: Mountaineers, Miners, and Indians
Traces of Ozarks Past: Outlaws, Icons, and Memorable Events

Cover photo by Seth N. Jackson.

All rights reserved. No part of this book may be reproduced or transmitted in any form or by any means, electronic or mechanical, including photocopying, recording or by any information storage and retrieval system without written permission from the author, except for the inclusion of brief quotations in a review.

International Standard Book Numbers
Paperbound: 978-0-7884-5710-4
Clothbound: 978-0-7884-6424-9

CONTENTS

1...Irishwoman Nellie Cashman: Prospecting "Angel" from Tucson to the Yukon
9...Colorado's Horace and "Baby Doe" Tabor: Silver King and Queen
17...Zebulon Pike: Soldier, Explorer, and Icon
23...Daniel Boone, a "Long Hunter"
31...Jedediah Smith: The "Westering" Mountain Man
37...Sequoya: Cherokee Syllabary Inventor
43...Black Hills Betrayal and the Last Stand
49...John Colter: Missouri's Legendary Mountain Man
57...Bullies, Wovoka, and the Massacre at Wounded Knee Creek
65...John Louis O'Sullivan and the "Manifest Destiny" Expansion Crusade
71...John Augustus Sutter and the California Gold Rush
79...Bent's Fort: Colorado's Adobe Oasis
85...Famed Custer and the Bloody Washita Massacre
91...Nathan Boone: Soldier, Surveyor, and Mountaineer
97...Promontory Point: Iron Trail from Coast to Coast
103...Ruff and Romantic Era of the Stagecoach and Pony Express
111..."Black Bart": California's Poetic Highwayman
117...Oklahoma Indian Territory: The Final Frontier
123...Jim Bridger: Solving Western Mysteries

Introduction

BEFORE the arrival of the Europeans to America there were about 10,000,000 native inhabitants that populated the continent. As the whites sailed across the Atlantic to the Eastern Seaboard in increasing numbers, the American Indian was forced to give up ground and move ever westward—their bows and arrows were, for the most part, no match against the eventual volleys of musket-fire sprayed upon them from the greedy, land-hungry colonists, U.S. army, and early settlers.

After the Louisiana Purchase in 1803 that doubled the size of the United States, President Thomas Jefferson's "Corps of Discovery" expedition of exploration of Meriwether Lewis and William Clark, set the stage for robust western conquest and ventures. The icing on the cake, however, would come thanks to John L. O'Sullivan in 1845 when he coined the clever phrase-machine "Manifest Destiny" in the *Democratic Review*, which quickly became a useful tool and slogan for expansion. It inspired a nation of real estate-grabbing, white Americans who believed that God had given them permission to take control of North America from coast to coast. As a result, war with Native Americans and Mexicans followed. From 1866 to 1890 about 45,000 Indians were reportedly killed during the expansionist period.

Overtime, with the discovery of gold in places like Sutter's Mill on January 24, 1848, the "Great Migration" was under way and in full swing. The first wagon trains, however, began in 1830 when two mountain men, Jedediah Strong Smith and William Sublette, led a group across the Rocky Mountains through the South Pass and proved the 500-mile journey to the West Coast was possible. Such trips were not without dangers, about one-tenth of the brave pioneers that went west on the Oregon Trail perished en route and were laid to rest in common graves along the dusty trace; other trails, such as the Bozeman, Santa Fe, and California were also utilized.

Many of the westward-bound trains faced multitudes of hardships, including Indian attacks. The problem was easily solved according to General Philip H. Sheridan, who said that there were about 100,000,000 buffaloes roaming the countryside from Fort Dodge, Kansas, to the Indian Nations (Oklahoma). Colonel Grenville Dodge reported in 1856 that he had seen thunderous herds of bison fifty miles wide and ten miles long. Gen. Sheridan's solution to the Indian problem was the extermination of the buffalo; he preached that by killing them the Plains Indians would have no means to continue their way of life. By 1889, less than 600 American bison remained.

Massacres and disputes led to the deaths of many Native Americans, like the Massacre of Sand Creek in Colorado, Massacre of Washita in Oklahoma, and Wounded Knee in South Dakota. One killing-field took place on August 3, 1832, at the Bad Axe River in Wisconsin. Whites in present-day Illinois and Wisconsin were squabbling over land with the Sauk and Fox Indians who had ceded to the United States about 50,000,000 acres of land—part of present-day Wisconsin, Missouri, and northwestern Illinois. The problem was that Sauk Chief Black Hawk eventually rejected the treaty as a fraud to his people, so he decided to stay on the land. After a number of deadly raids, Black Hawk and his followers were eventually driven back into present-day Iowa. As a result, Black Hawk gathered together about 400 braves and their families and defiantly went into Illinois to live and plant crops in the fertile soil. This was unacceptable to the whites, so regulars under General Henry Atkinson and the state militia under General Whiteside, along with the armed ship *Warrior*, and some Sioux Indians, made plans to confront Black Hawk and order him and his people to return to Iowa. Outgunned, Black Hawk made talk of peace, but it fell on deaf ears; and one of Black Hawk's envoys was killed. The Indians, of course, retaliated, which caused Gen. Atkinson to take his force of about 1,300 soldiers to the Bad Axe River where they massacred the hostile followers of Black Hawk; many of the casualties were women and children attempting to retreat across the river.

From the mountaineers that braved the elements and dangers in the West, to the wagon trains, steamboats, transcontinental railroad and other modern innovations, American expansion was eventually realized. Prospectors by the thousands would go on to roam the West from the border of Mexico to Alaska and the Klondike. Many discovered gold and made their fortunes, while many others had only their dreams to satisfy their hunger for wealth and prosperity. As for the Native Americans, they witnessed their precious land of milk and honey disappearing before their very eyes.

The stories and tales of those early American birth-pangs of the Wild West will forever be worthwhile and timeless—destined to be retold and revisited time and again. RTJ

Timeless Stories of the West
Mountaineers, Miners, and Indians

Irishwoman Nellie Cashman: Prospecting "Angel" from Tucson to the Yukon

THE HOPE of striking it rich and living the "easy" life was a magnet for many 19th century individuals who responded to the news of the abundance of silver and gold being found in the West. The wild and wooly lifestyle, which offered freedoms and opportunities unfettered by the rules and regulations enforced in communities that were less remote, was also a temptation for some to go westward—and go wild. In the Western expanse there was opportunity for a multitude of possibilities, and it bewitched the spirits and souls of many to dream the dream. It was the belief of John L. O'Sullivan, editor of the *United States Magazine and Democratic Review*, who wrote in 1845 that it was our "Manifest Destiny"—will of God, to control and take over all of North America; many others probably shared in O'Sullivan's type of faith. There was at least one woman, as brave, tough, and daring as any man alive who migrated to the American West and went on to become a North American legend. Her eventful life and times is a treasure trove for anyone interested in 19th century history and the Old West.

Nellie (Ellen) Cashman was born in Midleton, County Cork, Ireland in October 1845, at a time when the potato famine was still prompting many Irish to relocate elsewhere. The famished Irish suffered on account of the blight and many migrated to America; for example, about 75,000 in 1845 and about 106,000 in 1846. Midleton, where Nellie's birth is recorded, is located near Queenstown; the town was named Queenstown in 1849 after Queen Victoria graced the community with a visit; however, in 1922 it was renamed Cobh. Large numbers of Irish immigrants departed from this bustling seaport bound for new lives in America. They left behind the beautiful south-facing cliffs of the "Emerald Isle's" County Cork and headed for the unknown trials and tribulations of a Western migration.

Accompanying Nellie on her transatlantic voyage to America was her widowed mother Frances and her younger sister Fanny (some sources say Frances). They put down their roots in Boston, Massachusetts, where Nellie found honest employment as a hotel bellhop. As the story goes, while working there she met Union General Ulysses S. Grant who encouraged her to head west. Sometime in the mid-to-late 1860s, for whatever the reason, Nellie and her mother and sister headed for America's West Coast and settled in San Francisco, California. Like many before them, throngs of pioneers traveled west and crossed the Rocky Mountains and took the California Trail to Sacramento; others journeyed by sea around Cape Horn, South America, or crossed overland at the Isthmus of Panama—this was before the construction of the Panama Canal. The transcontinental railroad wasn't completed until 1869.

About California gold miners and the California Gold Rush, which began after James Marshall discovered gold in the sawmill race at John Sutter's Mill on the American River at Coloma, California on January 24, 1848, one historian had this to say: "These men ought to be as well known in song and story as the Greek Argonauts for their quest of the Golden Fleece, for the Forty-Niners were the American Argonauts who showed the worth of our far West to the world...The American Argonauts found their real Golden Fleece in the farms, pastures, herds, orchards, and democratic homes of the sunset land."

Not long after the "boom" and "stampede" of the 1840s which led prospectors to search for precious metals from Arizona to the Yukon, wild tales of plentiful gold in Colorado brought as many as a 100,000 "Fifty-Niners" to the state. "'Pikes Peak or Bust' was painted on many a wagon crossing the prairies. The machinery necessary for mining the gold and extracting it from the ore was so expensive that more than half the Fifty-Niners came back. On many a returning wagon might be seen the scrawl 'Busted.'

"This second great rush for gold gave people more knowledge of the interior West and showed that it was a good place in which to settle. It also made plain the necessity of extending the railroads to the far West."

Living in the West soon gave Nellie's sister Fanny the opportunity to meet and wed Thomas J. Cunningham, an Irish immigrant. While in San Francisco Nellie got "wind" of a rich strike in Nevada, known as the "Comstock," so she followed her instincts to Pioche, Nevada in 1872 and opened up a boarding house to cater to the miners; she also did prospecting herself and managed to amass a small fortune which enabled her to invest in other area businesses and to help others in need—the rowdy town of Pioche boasted 72 saloons and 32 brothels to keep the riff-raff entertained.

Always ready and vulnerable to any news of a big strike, a few years later in 1874 boom-loving Cashman headed north to the Cassiar District of British Columbia where she panned for gold along the Stikine River and into its tributaries. She became the first white female to live and work, for the most part, side-by-side with brawny men using her own handmade mining tools. A "placer" mining technique is described in *Little Journeys to Alaska and Canada* in this way: "A miner takes his pick, shovel and pan and goes, sometimes all alone, digging and picking in the creeks and rivers. He [or she] lifts up a pan of sand and looks anxiously for the glistening grains of gold. He rinses and rinses the sand. By skillful dipping he finally gets all of the sand out and has only the gold in the bottom of the pan. Sometimes he will find flakes as big as a pumpkin seed."

Taking her profits to Victoria, British Columbia, Cashman bought a boardinghouse and also generously helped to fund the St. Joseph Hospital. Her true, generous nature was best shown, however, after hearing about her comrade miners back in the Cassair District who were snowed-in and suffering from scurvy. Cashman's next adventure to save these fellow prospectors would earn her the sobriquets (nicknames) like "Saint of the Sourdoughs," the "Angel of Cassair," "Miner's Angel" and others.

Cashman hired six men, and with a variety of medical supplies, vegetables, and lime juice—about 1,500 pounds of provisions in all, loaded on pack animals, they trudged on towards the destitute mining camp. Even the reluctant Canadian army attempted to dissuade the group from making the dangerous wintertime rescue; however, Cashman was relentless and despite the warnings continued on for seventy-seven days. When the party finally reached the Cassair diggings, they found and saved the lives of seventy grateful men. Newspapers heralded the dangerous, epic endeavor and praised the brave and daring 31-year-old Irishwoman for her amazing efforts of mercy.

Whether Cashman had her belly full of cold weather or not, is uncertain, but in 1879 she headed south and didn't stop until she had reached Tucson, Arizona Territory. Before long she had opened an eatery called the Delmonico Restaurant—while, of course, keeping her ears open for any prospecting prospects. After a silver strike in nearby Tombstone by Ed Schiefflin was made public, Cashman quickly high-tailed it out of Tucson and lit-out for Tombstone where she invested in a couple more eateries and a mercantile store—always the entrepreneur.

Tombstone was a wild and wooly town full of gamblers, gunslingers, outlaws, and other such characters, which opened the door to men like Wyatt Earp and "Doc" Holiday—and, eventually the famous shoot-out at the OK Corral on October 26, 1881. Deputy Marshall Wyatt Earp and his brothers, Virgil, and Morgan, along with Doc Holiday, gunned down Tom McLowry, Frank McLowry, and Billy Clanton; however, Ike Clanton escaped—the battle lasted about thirty seconds.

While Cashman was in Tombstone she led an effort to establish a hospital and Catholic church, as well as helping "soiled doves" and the town's Irish Land League; and all of this while not forsaking her true passion—wandering the hillsides for coveted silver. On July 3, 1883, Nellie's sister died and she became the legal guardian of her five children which she eventually placed in Catholic boarding schools.

Irishwoman Nellie Cashman

Word of gold in the Baja region of Mexico and California enticed Cashman to organize a twenty-two-man prospecting party to traverse about 1,000 miles in their quest. They reached Guaymas, Mexico on May 24, 1883; and the Mission Santa Gertrudis. While out working in the boiling desert sun of the Golo Valley, their water ran low and Nellie stepped up and volunteered to go for help and supplies. Before long, she had returned with everything they needed to make their way back to civilization. Cashman was heralded yet again for her bravery and dubbed the "Frontier Angel."

Once, when a wooden-framed grandstand was constructed for the purpose of an admission-charging hanging spectacle of five condemned men in the town of Bisbee, Cashman, who didn't believe it was acceptable for such a thing to be turned into entertainment, sprang into action and dismantled the bleachers and earned still another nickname, the "Angel of Tombstone."

In 1896 the cry of gold in the Yukon prompted the Irishwoman to eventually leave the heat of the Arizona Territory and head north. By February 15, 1898, she had reached Skagway, Alaska. Concerning 19th century Skagway, one visitor observed that: "…all about the buildings and sides of the mountains the trees are bleached almost white from the fumes of the smoke rising from the works which are in operation day and night."

In order to reach the Yukon gold field "bonanza" near the mining town of Dawson City, Alaska, which had sprung up like a mushroom—located at the Yukon and Klondike river confluence, Cashman had to traverse the treacherous Chilkoot Pass and travel the Yukon River; she arrived in "Dawson" by April 1898. By the end of the year about 25,000 "placer" mining prospectors had populated the area; the first alluvial gold was discovered on August 17, 1896, in Bonanza Creek, a tributary of the Klondike River. The population during Dawson's peak swelled to about 40,000.

About working in the Yukon, miners had to "walk or use sledges and dogs. This is what the miners are obliged to do who carry on mining in the Klondike region…For the summers are short and the ground is frozen two-thirds of the year. Fires must be built on the ground to thaw the earth before it can be dug up.

"When the spring comes and the ice melts in the streams the

TIMELESS STORIES OF THE WEST

Northwest Territory, Alaska, on the way to the Klondike.

(From: *Little Journeys to Alaska and Canada*, Marian M. George, A. Flanagan Company, Chicago, Illinois, 1901.)

miners take advantage of the running water to wash out the gold from the earth they have carried and piled up along the banks...These miners suffer great hardships in order to wring their living from the soil, and many of them die of hunger and cold."

For the next several years Cashman panned gold and used her accumulated wealth to invest in the restaurant business in Dawson and continued to help others less fortunate. Nellie's mother, Frances, died in San Francisco in 1899. By 1904, Cashman once again heard the "call of the wild" and headed for a new gold strike in Fairbanks, Alaska. She sought riches near the Artic Circle from the Koyukuk River region to Cold Foot and finally in the Nolan Creek area along the Brooks Mountain Range. And last but not least at the ripe old age of seventy, Cashman mushed a team of dogs and sledded 700-750 frozen miles from Koyukuk to Seward, which took seventeen hard-fought days and earned her yet another name to add to her portfolio of achievements: Champion Woman Musher. A few months later after suffering from pneumonia she passed away on January 4, 1925, ironically, at the St. Joseph Hospital in Victoria, British Columbia—the facility she helped establish years earlier. Nellie Cashman, the brave, daring, caring Irishwoman from County Cork, Ireland, was laid to rest at the Ross Bay Cemetery (Victoria) alongside her sister, Fanny. Any future news of gold strikes and possible rushes, booms, and stampedes, would have to go on without their Irish angel.

TIMELESS STORIES OF THE WEST

Bibliography

Athearn, Robert G., *American Heritage New Illustrated History of the United States*, Volume 6, *The Frontier*, Fawcett Publishing, Inc., New York, N.Y., 1963.

Dungan, Myles, *How the Irish Won the West*, Skyhorse Publishing, Inc., 2011.

Enss, Chris, *A Beautiful Mine: Women Prospectors of the Old West*, TwoDot, Globe Pequot Press, Guilford, Connecticut, 2008.

Funk & Wagnalls New Encyclopedia, Funk & Wagnalls, Inc., New York, 1979.

George, Marian M., *Little Journeys to Alaska and Canada*, A. Flanagan Company, Chicago, Illinois, 1901.

Halleck, Reuben Post, *History of Our Country*, American Book Company, 1923.

Lalor, Brian, *The Encyclopedia of Ireland*, Yale University Press, New Haven and London, 2003.

Legrand, Jacques, *Chronicle of America*, Chronicle Publications, Inc., 1989.

Mayo, Matthew P., *Sourdoughs, Claim Jumpers, & Dry Gulchers: Fifty of the Grittiest Moments in the History of Frontier Prospecting*, TwoDot, Globe Pequot Press, Guilford, Connecticut, 2012.

Raine, William MacLeod, *Famous Sheriffs and Western Outlaws: Incredible True Stories of Wild West Showdowns and Frontier Justice*, Skyhorse Publishing, Inc., 2012.

Colorado's Horace and "Baby Doe" Tabor: Silver King and Queen

IN THE 1840s, ruff, tough, and rugged individuals, many of them were Welsh, Irish, and Cornish immigrants that brought mining expertise with them from their homelands, flocked to the gold fields of California. Along with these "forty-niners" came others as well, and "every new discovery of placers or veins had drawn its crowd of gamblers and desperadoes to the ephemeral [transient] mining camps."

It didn't take long before gold was also discovered in Cherry Creek, Colorado, in 1858; however, the region wasn't officially designated Colorado Territory until February 28, 1861; and later, Colorado became the 38th state on August 1, 1876, and was dubbed the "Centennial State" because it was admitted 100 years after the signing of the Declaration of Independence. John L. Routt, a Union veteran of the American Civil War, became the state's first governor. Denver was named the capital and "within the next two or three years scores of thousands of people flocked to this new El Dorado. Denver sprang from a stage station to a city, it might almost be said, in a night. A line of alleged cities arose along the east base of the mountains...."

The rush for precious metals caused problems when a spirit of greed possessed many whites to covet Indian land. Even before the War Between the States had ended in 1865, aggressive whites of

Colorado wanted to take what didn't belong to them. The United States government had recently guaranteed the Cheyenne and Arapahos the Sand Creek Reservation lands near Fort Lyons, as well as the promise of protection. On a chilly, dark morning, November 29, 1864, while about six hundred Native Americans camping along Sand Creek slept, cuddled together—mostly women, children, and old men, a wild-for-blood detachment of soldiers descended upon them.

The blood-thirsty gang of barroom ruffians and other Denver lowlifes was led by Colonel John Chivington, a Christian, Methodist minister; and his loyal disciples were Colorado Volunteers. These "wolves in sheep's clothing" were armed, though, with death-dealing howitzers and rifles, and they had anything but "love thy neighbor" on their hearts and minds. To make matters worse, the leader of the tribes was Black Kettle, a man of peace and accommodation; and flapping proudly in the breeze above the camp was America's "Stars and Stripes"—and also a white flag of truce.

It made little or no difference to Chivington's faithful flock bent on killing the heathens. Soon, more than two hundred souls were taken without mercy or warning—they were assaulted, scalped, brained, mutilated, and gutted—while taking grisly souvenirs. The remaining victims of the Sand Creek Massacre having learned from their white brethren how to do it, went on a series of their own killing sprees in retaliation through parts of Kansas, Nebraska, Wyoming, and Colorado. This probably made the Indians "fair game" to the delight of many.

Some white citizens actually believed that this sort of ungodly behavior was justified in order to better pursue their future opportunities and happiness in the Western frontier—"Manifest Destiny." Though the news media made an attempt to condemn Col. Chivington's barbaric crimes—it, reportedly went unpunished. Afterwards, who knows, butcher-minister Chivington might have returned to his pulpit—with his faithful followers behind him.

With Colorado now wide-open for the conquest of untold riches and wealth, in 1877 large deposits of silver was discovered in the Centennial State and once more "tens of thousands of fortune seekers rushed to the diggings. Stray Horse Gulch, which was

Colorado's Horace and "Baby Doe" Tabor

Photo of Colorado captured and provided by Seth N. Jackson.

decorated with about a score of miners' shanties left by the receding wave of a decade before, grew in a few months into the city of Leadville...."

With the stage now set for a Colorado "Silver King," Horace Austin Warner Tabor who started out in Vermont in the grocery business and as a part-time postmaster, made the decision to relocate to the wild and wooly West during the gold rush of the 1850s; Tabor, along with his wife, Augusta, crossed the Great Plains in an ox-drawn wagon in 1859 and landed in the Leadville, Colorado area. Tabor would go on to become a very wealthy and successful man; first, he panned a fortune in gold at Gregory Gulch; and next, he grubstaked a couple of miners, August Rische and George Hook, in the Little Pittsburgh Silver Mine, after which Tabor sold his share about a year later for a "cool" million—a lot of money in those days.

Overtime the town of Leadville continued to grow by leaps and bounds and boasted, besides a number of newspapers, banks, schools and churches, scores of saloons, gambling joints, and bordellos; and many other things also sprang up to satisfy the flourishing community. Tabor would serve as the town mayor and postmaster; he also once served as the governor of Colorado.

With some of his fortune, Tabor laid claim to his pride and joy, the Matchless Mine. The "Matchless" was a money-maker and before long Tabor had built a couple of opera houses, one in Leadville and one in Denver; he also invested in a number of mines in southwestern states as well as other investments in Latin America. Tabor liked to dabble in politics and gave large contributions to the Republican Party, expecting some favors and support in return. One of the most pivotal moments in Tabor's eventful life, however, came by chance one day at the opera when his gaze met that of a young lady who had her eyes set on a life of wealth and high-class citizenry. Almost overnight, Tabor had turned his back on the old and embraced his new love-interest who would become well-known as the good looking "Baby Doe"—and eventually, the "Silver Queen."

Elizabeth Bonduel McCourt was born in 1854 in Oshkosh, Wisconsin, a town located in the east-central part of the state on the west bank of Lake Winnebago. Her parents, on the other hand, were immigrants from County Armagh, Ireland, a southern Ulster and Northern Ireland border county. The people who lived in County Armagh had shared in the suffering of the Great Famine and potato blight that plagued the "Emerald Isle" in the 19th century, which forced many Irish to consider relocation. As a result, many migrated to America and to the reported opportunities that awaited them there—especially in the West.

Elizabeth was born with natural beauty and learned at an early age how to utilize it on her male counterparts to get whatever she wanted. One winter Elizabeth competed in a church skating contest and won the lustful attention of a well-to-do mining heir, Harvey Doe. The two tied-the-knot about a year later on June 27, 1877, and headed out West to Central City, Colorado, where her new husband worked the Fourth of July Mine; however, wealth did not come easily and the "honeymoon" was short-lived, dissolving their marriage in 1880. Elizabeth left Central City behind and moved on to Leadville and her meeting with Horace Tabor, the Silver King.

After Baby Doe met Horace at the opera house they quickly began a "whirlwind" romance, and after his divorce from Augusta was finalized, they had a church-marriage on March 1, 1883. For several years they lived the "life of Riley" and enjoyed luxury and a rich lifestyle—but, all good things must come to an end and, in 1893 the repeal of the Sherman Silver Purchase Act caused the bottom to fall out of the market and little-by-little Horace and Baby Doe lost everything; the only thing they managed to save was their beloved Matchless Mine. As a result of their financial ruin, Horace had to swallow his pride and return to menial labor in a mine that once belonged to him. The loss of their social status and wealth was devastating to Baby Doe. Horace eventually became the postmaster in Denver, for a spell, but finally died on April 3, 1899.

In 1891, another gold strike in Colorado in the Crede and Cripple Creek area brought thousands more to search for riches. The discovery was made by accident when a cowboy named Bob Womack found some of the precious, sought-after metal. Saloons, theaters, banks, hotels and all the other things that made up a boomtown community in the Old West were created in a short time.

The golden days waned and the "...placers were quickly worked out under the wasteful system, or lack of system, which was pursued, and the greater part of the adventurers left the Territory to skim the cream from other mining regions, Nevada and Montana."

After the loss of Horace, despite all of Baby Doe's best mining efforts, the Matchless Mine never came to her rescue nor cared about her feminine wiles; even her two daughters abandoned her to her precious failing mine—Elizabeth Lillie Tabor went back to Wisconsin and Rose ("Silver Dollar") Tabor moved to Chicago, Illinois, and was reportedly found dead, but not before she had changed her name to Ruth Norman.

Baby Doe was eventually forced to sell the Matchless Mine in 1927; however, she was allowed to remain in a small cabin located near the mine. A hard, cold winter would take a toll on Baby Doe and she passed away on February 20, 1935. She was found all alone, frozen on the cabin floor and had probably been dead for about a week. Baby Doe was taken to the Mount Olivet Cemetery in Wheat Ridge, Colorado, and buried next to Horace. Afterwards, their legacy continued from beyond the grave in newspapers, magazines, songs, and also in an opera titled *The Ballad of Baby Doe* which played as late as 1956.

Whether or not Colorado's King and Queen of Silver ever stored any of their treasure in heaven will probably never be known here on earth—but, one thing is certain, while they were alive the Tabors did their share of prospecting during those historic, frontier mining days of the American West.

Bibliography

Barnard, Edward S., *Story of the Great American West*, The Reader's Digest Association, Inc., Pleasantville, New York, 1977.

Dungan, Myles, *How the Irish Won the West*, Skyhorse Publishing, New York, N.Y., 2011.

Enss, Chris, *More Tales Behind the Tombstones: More Deaths and Burials of the Old West's Most Nefarious Outlaws, Notorious Women, and Celebrated Lawmen*, TwoDot, Rowland & Littlefield, Guilford, Connecticut, 2015.

Funk & Wagnalls New Encyclopedia, Funk & Wagnalls, Inc., New York, 1979.

Goldfield, David, *The American Journey: A History of the United States*, Prentice Hall, Upper Saddle River, New Jersey, 1998.

Kreck, Dick, *Hell on Wheels: Wicked Towns along the Union Pacific Railroad*, Fulcrum Publishing, Golden, Colorado, 2013.

Lalor, Brian, *The Encyclopedia of Ireland*, Yale University Press, New Haven and London, 2003.

Legrand, Jacques, *Chronicle of America*, Chronicle Publications, Inc., Mount Kisco, New York, 1989.

Mayo, Matthew P., *Sourdoughs, Claim Jumpers & Dry Gulchers: Fifty of the Grittiest Moments in the History of Frontier Prospecting*, TwoDot, Globe Pequot Press, Guilford, Connecticut, 2012.

Muzzey, David Saville, *The United States of America: II From the Civil War*, Ginn and Company, Boston, 1924.

Zebulon Pike:
Soldier, Explorer, and Icon

EARLY IN THE 19th century a vast majority of the West was, for the most part, wild, wooly, and unexplored. The Louisiana Purchase, a 909,000-square-mile chunk of real estate, was acquired from France in 1803 for the bargain price of $15 million which doubled the size of the United States of America; it was considered one of the greatest land deals of all time. As a result, that same year President Thomas Jefferson deployed Captain Meriwether Lewis, a former personal secretary and aide-de-camp to the president, and Captain William Clark, an old friend of Lewis', to undertake a perilous expedition known as the "Corps of Discovery." Within 18 months the Lewis and Clark party had traversed almost 4,000 miles from St. Louis, Missouri, to the Pacific Ocean. By the time the heralded group of explorers had returned to St. Louis, 28 months had expired.

Soon after the success of Lewis and Clark, other important, lesser-known expeditions were mounted—first, to explore the Upper Mississippi River and, secondly, venture into the southwest portion of the newly acquired Louisiana Territory to seek out the headwaters of the Arkansas and Red Rivers. The exploits of these historic journeys would, ironically, be published before those of the more famous Lewis and Clark.

Zebulon Montgomery Pike was born in Trenton, New Jersey, in

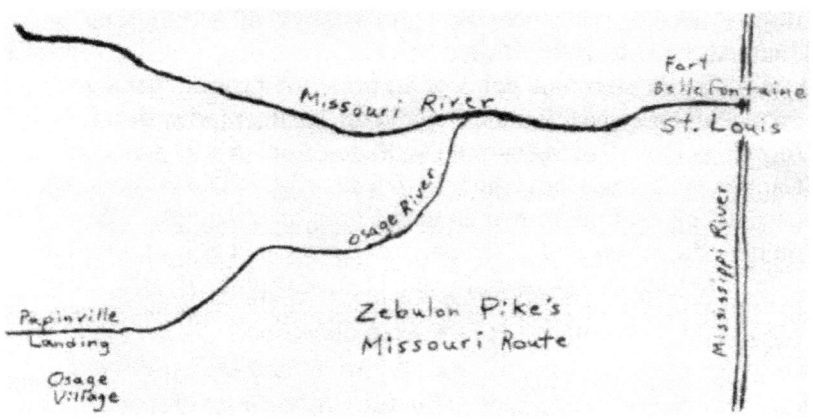

Above: A mural in downtown Butler, Mo. Below: An illustration of Pike's journey through Missouri to the Papinville Landing.

Zebulon Pike

1779. He joined the United States army in 1793 and had attained the rank of second lieutenant by 1799. As a loyal follower of General James Wilkinson the governor of Missouri Territory, Wilkinson naturally selected Lieut. Pike to explore the Upper Mississippi.

Pike, along with twenty-two other soldiers and a 70-foot keelboat, set out from Fort Bellefontaine and St. Louis, Missouri, on August 9, 1805. Pike's mission was to, besides locate the source of the mighty river, extend Federal authority and sovereignty over Native Americans and attempt to "warn off" fur trappers from Canada.

Traveling north, Pike visited the lead mines of Julien Dubuque and the French settlement of Prairie du Chien where he reminded the English and French traders there about U.S. laws and regulations—they were not at all amused or receptive to the idea.

In Minnesota, Pike parleyed with the Sioux for a military campsite and reservation of one hundred thousand acres at the Minnesota and Mississippi River confluence area for 60 gallons of whiskey and a few hundred dollars of other goods of trade. The promised fort, Indian agency, and factory trading house, however, were not established there until 1819.

At Little Falls, Minnesota, Pike and his men built a small, square stockade as a winter quarters. On December 10 Pike took half his party and set out on a long, cold journey to discover the Mississippi's northernmost source. Suffering from frostbite—toes and fingers—they found some care and refuge at Canadian and British trading posts scattered along the way. Eventually, they reached Leech Lake, which Pike believed was the great river's main point of origin; however, it was later learned that a bit further to the west was the true source of the Mississippi River at Lake Itasca.

After Pike's triumphal return to St. Louis on April 30, 1806, he was again chosen by Gen. Wilkinson for a second mission into the vast regions of the southwest Louisiana Purchase. On July 15, Lieut. Pike left St. Louis with a party of twenty-three other men traveling up the Missouri River in two barges; also in their group were fifty-one Osage and Pawnee Indians which they were escorting back to their villages in southwest Missouri—redeemed from captivity. Reaching the Osage River, they rowed and poled the boats along while the Indians walked beside the water's edge. Following the river through Missouri, Pike commented about the beauty of it and the prairies that were "crowned" with a wealth of "luxuriant" grasses.

When Pike arrived at the Papinville Landing near the "Grand" and "Little" Osage in what is now the southeastern part of Bates County, Mo., he established Camp Independence. When the Indian hostages were returned upon their arrival, the Osage chief, Sans Oreille, overwhelmed with surprise and joy about the turn of events, told his people that the Americans had "stretched out their hands, and they are returned to you! What can you do in return for all this goodness? Nothing: all your lives would not suffice to repay their goodness." While there, Pike noted that the Big Osage had 214 lodges, about 500 warriors, 852 women, and 341 children; the Little Osage numbered a total of about 824 souls.

Lieut. Pike "struck" camp on September 1, 1806, and headed further to the west (Kansas) and the Pawnee village on the Republican River. Pike's mission was to make peace with them, as he had with the Osage, and to impart American influence upon the Pawnee people.

Venturing up the Arkansas River they discovered a "grand mountain peak" in the southern reaches of the Rocky Mountains near present-day Pueblo, Colorado, which Pike compared to a "small blue cloud," and they proceeded, unsuccessfully, to climb it—only reaching the pinnacle of Cheyenne Mountain. Afterwards, Pike declared the mountain so rugged that it was an impossible challenge for anyone to climb. Pathfinder John Charles Fremont would later, in the mid-1800s, dub the mountaintop "Pike's Peak."

Leaving the Colorado mountain range behind Pike's company headed south, possibly to escape the cold November weather that had unexpectedly befallen them, where nine of them suffered with frozen feet. As a result of their turn to the south, however, they had trespassed into Spanish territory and were arrested in February 1807 and taken to Santa Fe, New Mexico. The governor decided to have them escorted under guard to Chihuahua, Mexico, through what is now the state of Texas, and consequently on to Natchitoches (Louisiana) which they reached on July 1, 1807. During the trek his maps and writings were confiscated, but not to be denied, he managed to save some by hiding them in the unloaded muzzleloader-barrels of his company. The precious documents helped Pike to remember his experiences in the West enough to publish his findings in 1810—on the other hand, Clark's journals *The History of the Expeditions of Captains Lewis and Clark* were not published until 1814. After the mysterious death of Meriwether Lewis in 1809, editors Paul Allen and Nicholas Biddle utilized the notes of Lewis and Clark to complete the book, which may have added to its later publishing date to that of Pike's.

Pike's views of the Great American Desert and Plains as suitable for only Native Americans would help to cast a shadow in the minds of many for a number of years, which hampered robust settlement of the West. However, Pike's tales of Missouri, Western wildlife, breathtaking mountains, rivers and streams, and the woodlands of the Western Territory, stirred the imagination of pioneers and American expansionists greedy for more. Eventually, hosts of daring individuals also ventured west along the Santa Fe and Oregon Trails to overcome the myth of the treeless plains and inhabitable desert land that was first reported by Pike.

In November, during the War of 1812, Colonel Zebulon Pike marched on Montreal, Canada, with about 600 men and attacked the fort, which was unknowingly occupied by Americans. Because of the blunder, there were about 50 casualties.

Then, in April 1813 while capturing York, Canada, Brigadier General Zebulon Pike was killed when retreating British troops blew up the main powder magazine to keep it from falling into enemy hands; about 300 other Americans were also killed or wounded in the deadly blast.

The many exploits of Zebulon Pike as a soldier and explorer never, for some reason, elevated his historical status and significance to Thomas Jefferson's team of Lewis and Clark; nevertheless, history does remember Pike on occasion and his honorable name rises to the surface where he takes his place among the early mountaineers and pathfinders as a prominent figure of the American West.

TIMELESS STORIES OF THE WEST

Bibliography

Athearn, Robert G., *American Heritage: New Illustrated History of the United States*, Vol. 6, *The Frontier*, Fawcett Publications, Inc. One Astor Plaza, New York, N.Y., 1963.

Chronicle of America, Chronicle Publications, Mount Kisco, New York, 1989.

Coit, Margaret L., *The Growing Years*, Vol. 3, 1789-1829, Time-Life Books, New York, 1963.

Funk & Wagnalls New Encyclopedia, Funk & Wagnalls, Inc., New York, 1979.

Jackson, Rex T., *The Exploits of Zebulon Pike*, The Ozarks Reader Magazine, Vol. 7, No. 1, 2010.

Parrish, Jones, Jr., and Christensen, *Missouri: The Heart of the Nation*, Forum Press, Inc., Arlington Heights, Illinois, 1980.

Daniel Boone, a "Long Hunter"

THE WINNING of the West took a special breed of individuals, and they were known by such names as woodsmen, scouts, mountain men, explorers, riflemen, pioneers, Indian fighters, wagoneers, trappers, marksmen, guides, soldiers, pathfinders, frontiersmen, and the list goes on. At first, the wild and wooly American wilderness was home to Native Americans who viewed the whites as simply invaders; they believed the Great Father had given them the land and they were ready and willing to fight and die to keep it—and many of them did. Their tactics and culture was considered barbaric and savage; but consider, for example, the American Civil War where about 633,000 souls perished—brother against brother, over the heinous institution of slavery. Nevertheless, the West—and the nation, was won by men like Daniel Boone.

Daniel Boone was born in 1734 near Reading, Pennsylvania, into a family of Quakers at the headwaters of the Schuylkill River. In 1753 they relocated to what is now North Carolina in the Yadkin River Valley. Growing up in this region young Boone roamed the countryside hunting game and providing food for the table. In *The Adventures of Daniel Boone, the Kentucky Rifleman*, author Francis Lister Hawks writes: "He was scarcely able to carry a gun, when he was shooting all the squirrels, raccoons, and even wild-cats...he could find...."

It is said that he would carve messages on trees and boast about

TIMELESS STORIES OF THE WEST

Native American display at Har-Ber Village in Grove, Oklahoma.

his kills, saying such things as: "D Boon killed A bar heer." His spelling may be an indication of his lack of formal education, which was scant. As the story goes, he attended a log schoolhouse in the woods and had an Irish schoolmaster that was "sometimes good-humored, and then indulging the lads; sometimes surly and ill-natured, and then beating them severely."

It seems that while the children were out for recess the teacher would take a stroll; when he returned, however, and called the students in, his demeanor seemed to have changed and they were "whipped more severely and oftentimes without cause."

In order to solve the mystery, some of the older boys followed the schoolmaster during one of his walks and found that he had a sinister purpose for his daily exercise routine—in the form of a whiskey bottle. Boys will be boys and, as a result, they switched his bottle one day with a substitute one containing "tartar emetic" (a poisonous efforescent crystalline salt). This time the schoolmaster, after returning from his whiskey-walk, looked "pale and sick" but continued his work, calling on Daniel Boone to answer an arithmetic problem.

"If you take three quarters from a whole number, what remains?" asked the teacher. "The whole, sir," said Daniel. "You blockhead!" the schoolmaster retorted proceeding to physically abuse Daniel. Afterwards, young Daniel declared: "If I take one bottle of whiskey, and put in its place another in which I have mixed an emetic, the whole will remain, if nobody drinks it!" The old Irishman, "dreadfully sick," became enraged. He took hold of Daniel and started "beating him as the children shouted and roared." This ended Daniel Boone's short experience with his public education.

Daniel would eventually wed Rebecca Bryan and at the headwaters of North Carolina's Yadkin River, he too would put down roots, clear some land, build a log cabin for his new bride and plant crops. The Boone's had several children while other settlers continued to move in around them.

In 1755 Boone served as a wagoneer with British troops under General Edward Braddock in a raid on French-held Fort Duquesne during the French and Indian War; the expedition was unsuccessful.

The call of the wild continued to howl within Daniel's soul and one day he made up his mind to seek out Kentucky, or as the Iroquois Indians called it: "Ken-ta-ke," which means "great meadow." He began to explore the regions of Virginia, Tennessee, and Kentucky. About Kentucky and its future, in *Daniel Boone: His Own Story*, Boone describes in his own words his thoughts and opinions concerning it: "Thus we behold Kentucky, lately a howling wilderness, the habitation of savages and wild beasts, become a fruitful field...Here, where the hand of violence shed the blood of the innocent, where the horrid yells of savages and groans of the distressed sounded in our ears, we now hear the praises and adorations of our Creator; where wretched wigwams stood, the miserable abodes of savages, we behold the foundations of cites laid, that, in all probability, will equal the glory of the greatest upon earth."

Boone, like other "long hunters" who were away from home for long periods of time, left his family behind and along with John Finley, John Stewart, Joseph Holden, James Monay, and William Cool, ventured out through the Cumberland Gap and over the Blue Ridge Mountains to Kentucky. Between 1769 and 1771, the group explored the region and for the first time witnessed the thunderous herds of the American bison. The wonders Boone saw in Kentucky made him exclaim: "Who ever beheld such an abundance?"

Land-hungry citizens of Virginia and North Carolina would soon utilize the "Wilderness Road" that Boone and some 30 woodchoppers cut from Longisland, North Carolina, through the Allegheny Mountains to Otter Creek near a bend on the Kentucky River, where Boone built a stockade and fort on the site of what became the town of Boonesborough. In celebration of the town's first wedding which took place the same year of the Declaration of Independence, the people gathered around the flickering light of homemade candles made from buffalo tallow while they feasted on juicy, tasty watermelon—the fruits of their hard-earned labors. The settlement was guarded by palisades and blockhouses and completed by 1777, just in time for the many Indian attacks that would occur.

About such raids, Hawks wrote that "the sudden attack of the Indians was like a flash of lightning; they were seen only for an instant; yet, like the lightning they had done their work."

In 1778, Boone and 27 other men were captured by Chief Black Fish and his Shawnee warriors while they were at a salt lick about 40 miles north of Boonesborough. During the time Boone was with the Shawnee Indians he knew that if he attempted to escape "it would be certain death," so he pretended to be content. Apparently, he had taken the place of another brave who had been killed and was adopted into the tribe. Boone played along with his circumstances for a time, gaining favor with Chief Black Fish and the majority of the Shawnee people, until one day he saw his opportunity to escape and took flight. "He knew they would give chase, and therefore he doubled his track, waded in streams, and did everything he could to throw them off his trail...With no food but roots and berries, and scarcely time to devour these, he pushed through swamps and thickets for his home."

When Boone finally reached Boonesborough, the inhabitants couldn't believe their eyes—he was barefooted, clothed in Indian apparel and wearing a scalp lock. He had traveled about 160 miles in almost four days, bringing the news that Chief Black Fish and his Shawnee braves were on their way to attack the fort.

Boonesborough would be raided on many occasions, as Boone in his own words later wrote: "The barbarous savage nations of Shawanese, Cherokees, Wyandots, Tawas, Delawares, and several others...united in war against us."

According to Francis Hawks the settlers were in constant danger: "Indian massacres went on. Stories of savage butchery were heard of everywhere; every station that they dared approach felt their fury, and the poor settler who had built his cabin away from any station was sure to be visited."

The Boone family was no exception to the rule, and when their oldest son, James Boone, was captured by Indians, he was tortured to death. As a result, a gang of local settlers set out for revenge. They reportedly even the score by enticing some of the Mingo Indian tribe to drink, and in their drunken stupor the angry, deceptive settlers murdered and scalped them. It was also said that one of the Indian women who was with child, was chopped open by a tomahawk and the unborn baby impaled on a stake.

TIMELESS STORIES OF THE WEST

It was reported that between 1783 and 1790 about fifteen hundred Kentuckians were killed or captured. Many Native Americans also paid a high price as war with the settlers continued.

Despite his efforts and contributions to the Kentucky cause, in 1799, troubled with lawsuits over his Kentucky land claims, Boone decided that he'd had enough and declared that he wanted a little more "elbow room." So the 65-year-old mountaineer carved out a 60-foot yellow poplar canoe for his wife and children and pointed it in the direction of St. Louis, Missouri, and the Missouri River country (Spanish Territory); Boone and several others, however, traveled overland herding the livestock.

In 1803, the same year as the Louisiana Purchase which doubled the size of the United States, the 4-story Georgian-style Daniel Boone Home was begun near Defiance, Missouri, in the beautiful Femme Osage Valley; it was completed in 1810. Boone's land claim in Missouri was confirmed by the U.S. Congress in 1814, in recognition of his contributions to his country as an explorer and early pioneer.

For a couple decades the Boone family farmed, hunted, and blazed a path to Howard County and the salt licks located there along the Missouri River. Boone and his sons began to manufacture salt, and the road there became known as the "Boonslick Trail" or "Boone's Trace."

Daniel Boone died in 1820 in the Daniel Boone Home, which is now a historic site. A monument to him, the Daniel Boone Monument, is located in Marthasville, Mo., the site Boone selected for his and his wife Rebecca's final resting place, who was originally buried there. Years later, however, Daniel Boone was exhumed and reburied in the "Bluegrass State" of Kentucky—something he feared might happen; but some Missourians hold that Kentucky was given a substitute body and he is still at rest in Missouri. Whatever the case, his spirit will no doubt linger both east and west of the Mississippi River—as one of America's most famous trailblazers who spent much of his life away from home.

Daniel Boone, a "Long Hunter"

Chronology

1734—Daniel Boone is born near Reading, Pennsylvania.
1753—The Boone's relocate to present-day North Carolina in the Yadkin River Valley.
1755—Boone serves under British General Edward Braddock during the French and Indian War.
1769—Boone and five other men travel to Kentucky.
1777—the town of Boonesborough is completed.
1778—Boone is captured by Chief Black Fish and the Shawnee Indians.
1799—Boone decides to leave Kentucky and move west to the Spanish Territory near St. Louis, Missouri.
1803—The Louisiana Purchase doubles the size of the United States of America.
1810—The 4-story Daniel Boone Home is completed near Defiance, Missouri.
1814—U.S. Congress confirms Boone's Missouri land claims.
1820—Daniel Boone dies in the Daniel Boone Home.

TIMELESS STORIES OF THE WEST

Bibliography

Athearn, Robert G., *American Heritage New Illustrated History of the United States*, Vol. 6, *The Frontier*, Fawcett Publications, Inc., One Astor Plaza, New York, N.Y., 1963.

Boone, Daniel, *Daniel Boone: His Own Story*, Appleton, New York, 1844.

Chronicle of America, Chronicle Publications, Mount Kisco, N.Y., 1989.

Funk & Wagnalls New Encyclopedia, Funk & Wagnalls, Inc., New York, 1979.

Hawks, Francis Lister, *The Adventures of Daniel Boone, the Kentucky Rifleman*, Appleton, New York, 1844.

Jackson, Rex T., *James B. Eads: The Civil War Ironclads and His Mississippi*, Heritage Books, Inc., Bowie, Maryland, 2004.

Morris, Richard B., *The Making of a Nation*, Vol. 2, *1775-1789*, Time-Life Books, New York, 1963.

Jedediah Smith:
The "Westering" Mountain Man

AT ONE TIME the West was teeming with an abundance of animals to fuel the fur trading market. Across the vast expanse of the untamed Western portion of America, were treacherous mountains, deserts, rivers, and wooded country begging to be explored, conquered, and settled. Stories of unknown dangers and difficulties, too many to recount, litter those times in American history—of hairbreadth escapes from angry Indians, wild and hungry creatures, unpredictable weather, accidents, lack of food and water, and so on. The task was undertaken by daring mountain men, pathfinders, explorers, and fur trappers.

Jedediah Strong Smith was just such a man who was born in 1798 in Bainbridge, New York. In 1816 he moved to St. Louis, Missouri—the "gateway to the West." It is said that Jedediah was given a book about the expeditions of Meriwether Lewis and William Clark, which inspired his desire for "Westering." In 1822 Smith took notice of a newspaper advertisement searching for a hundred "enterprising young men" to participate in a trading venture masterminded by Lieutenant Governor William Henry Ashley and Major Andrew Henry; Ashley was a well-to-do businessman in St. Louis and Henry was an experienced fur trader.

Jedediah answered the call and became a member of the group. His first experience took him to Yellowstone where he was attacked and mauled by a grizzly bear; one of his ears was torn off in the battle with the beast and he was nearly killed. The party made

Traveling through a snow-covered mountain pass.
(From: *Little Journeys to Alaska and Canada*, Marian M. George, A. Flanagan Company, Chicago, Illinois, 1901.)

Jedediah Smith

friends at a Crow Indian village in the "Rockies" where they spent the winter. The South Pass was discovered in 1812 but its location was lost until Smith, with the help of a map he acquired from the Crow Indians, rediscovered the important route through America's Great Divide.

By 1824, Ashley and Henry's Rocky Mountain Fur Company had created the concept of a "rendezvous"-type trading business where trappers could bring in their catch of furs to a yearly trade fair, which they held in places like Green River and Jackson Hole, Wyoming. Eventually, Jedediah Smith and two other partners, Robert Campbell and William Sublette, bought the Rocky Mountain Fur Company and operated it until the late 1820s.

Robert Campbell was born on February 12, 1804, in County Tyrone (Contae Thir Eoghain), the largest county in Northern Ireland, to Hugh Campbell, Sr. and Elizabeth Buchanan (related to U.S. President James Buchanan). This part of the "Emerald Isle" boasts that eleven United States presidents have roots there: Andrew Jackson, James K. Polk, Andrew Johnson, James Buchanan, Ulysses S. Grant, Chester A. Arthur, Grover Cleveland, Benjamin Harris, William McKinley, Theodore Roosevelt, and Woodrow Wilson. Campbell departed Ireland in 1822 and crossed the Atlantic Ocean and moved overland to St. Louis, Mo. He traveled out West and met William Ashley who taught him all about the fur trading business. When Ashley retired Campbell teamed up with William Sublette, who also knew Ashley. When Campbell and Sublette retired from the fur business they opened the Sublette & Campbell store in St. Louis that sold a variety of goods, until it burned in 1849 in the town's Great Fire.

William Sublette heralded from Lincoln County, Kentucky and relocated to the St. Louis area in 1818. He established trading posts on the headwaters of the Missouri River and discovered a shortcut on the Oregon Trail that came to be known as "Sublette's Cutoff." Both Robert Campbell and William Sublette are buried at the beautiful Bellefontaine Cemetery in St. Louis, and are in good company with other such well-known Americans like: William Clark, James B. Eads, Henry Blow, Samuel Hawken, Sterling Price, Thomas Hart Benton, Emerson Gould, and many others.

TIMELESS STORIES OF THE WEST

From 1826 to 1830 Jedediah Smith blazed a trail throughout the American West. He traveled southwest with a party of sixteen other men from the Great Salt Lake up the Colorado River, down the western slopes of the southern Rocky Mountains and across the Mohave Desert to the Mission San Gabriel Arcangel, near present-day Los Angeles, California; the mission was founded in 1771 by Franciscan monks and is located just east of Los Angeles. In 1828 Smith and his expedition to Fort Vancouver, Washington, were attacked by a band of Indians near the Sacramento River in California. As a result, about 15 to 18 of his party were tomahawked and scalped in a vicious and savage hand-to-hand encounter; however, Smith somehow managed to "save his skin" by hightailing it into the wooded countryside. In the summer of 1830 Smith led a covered wagon train over the Rocky Mountains to the Upper Wind River, along with his partner, Sublette, of the Rocky Mountain Fur Company. Leaving the western reaches of the Missouri River region, the train traveled about 500 miles without incident through Indian country—the journey took about six weeks to complete.

Afterwards, the great mountain man made the decision to sell his interest in the Rocky Mountain Fur Company, which eventually merged with the Hudson Bay Company and the Northwest Company. By the 1840s much of the beaver population, due to the massive amount of trapping, had nearly been wiped out. It was also the same year that the last rendezvous of mountain men at Green River, Wyoming, was held.

The many rugged individuals that had scoured the mountainous West and mastered its geographical mysteries had inadvertently hastened the demise of their own way of life. Finally, in the summer of 1831, 33-year-old Jedediah Strong Smith, after he had invested in and joined a trading caravan to Santa Fe, was attacked and killed in a hopeless, outnumbered encounter with a Comanche hunting party at a watering hole near the Cimarron River on the Santa Fe Trail; however, the Comanche chief also died in the skirmish. Over the years many benefactors have walked and enjoyed the coveted ground beneath their feet—without getting to know, in many cases, those frontier trailblazers of the American West.

Jedediah Smith

Chronology

1798—Jedediah Strong Smith was born in Bainbridge, New York.
1816—Smith relocates to St. Louis, Missouri.
1822—Smith teams up with William Henry Ashley and Andrew Henry.
1824—Smith is attacked by a grizzly bear and nearly killed; the "rendezvous"-type trade fair is established.
1826—Smith crosses the southwest part of the continent to San Diego, California, to the Mission San Gabriel Arcangel.
1828—Smith and his party were attacked by Indians near the Sacramento River in California—15 to 18 were killed.
1830—Smith travels over the Rockies with a train of wagons to the Upper Wind River; the wagon train traveled 500 miles in six weeks.
1831—Jedediah Strong Smith was killed by a band of Comanche Indians on the Santa Fe Trail near the Cimarron River.

Bibliography

Amsler, Kevin, *Final Resting Place: The Lives and Deaths of Famous St. Louisians*, Virginia Publishing Company, St. Louis, Missouri, 1997.

Chronicle of America, Chronicle Publications, Mount Kisco, New York, 1989.

Dungan, Myles, *How the Irish Won the West*, Skyhorse Publishing, New York, N.Y., 2011.

Faragher, John Mack, *Out of Many: A History of the American People*, Prentice Hall, Upper Saddle River, New Jersey, 1994.

Funk & Wagnall New Encyclopedia, Funk & Wagnall, Inc., New York, 1979.

Golay, Michael; Bowman, John S., *North American Exploration*, John Wiley & Sons, Inc., Hoboken, New Jersey, 2003.

Insight Guides: Ireland, APA Publications, 2011.

Lalor, Brian, *The Encyclopedia of Ireland*, Gill & Macmillan, 2003.

Parrish, William E.; Jones, Jr., Charles T.; and Christensen, Lawrence O., *Missouri: The Heart of the Nation*, Forum Press, Inc., Arlington Heights, Illinois, 1980.

Sequoya:
Cherokee Syllabary Inventor

WESTERN TRAILBLAZERS were not always white; Native Americans also participated and became well-known icons of the American West. One such Cherokee, who rose to historical prominence, overcoming discouragement, ridicule, and numerous other obstacles, went on, in spite of it all, to pave the way to an honorable place at the table of history.

Sequoya (Sikwayi), or Sequoyah, was born in the Cherokee village of Tuskegee (Taskigi), Tennessee, near old Fort Loudon between 1760 and 1765; his Indian name means "Hog's Foot." Among the whites he was known as George Gist, or sometimes Guest or Guess. Most historians believe that his father, Nathaniel Gist, was a white fur trader from Virginia; and his mother, Wut-teh, was a mixed-blood daughter of a Cherokee chief. Sequoya eventually relocated to Georgia in the early 1800s and began to make silver ornaments, which led him to see how the white silversmiths would sign or letter their work. From this, and other things, he began to formulate ideas and plans for a Cherokee system of reading and writing.

As Sequoya was illiterate and never had the luxury of attending school throughout his lifetime, he "never learned to speak, read, or write the English language," according to James Mooney's *Myths of the Cherokee*. Nevertheless, he continued to dream the dream of a syllabary for his people—the same type of language that the whites had, which Native Americans called "talking leaf." They were

Likeness of Sequoya at the Will Rogers Memorial in Claremore, Oklahoma.

Sequoya

amazed and impressed by the words that could be stored on and spoken from a piece of paper.

After Sequoya served in the Creek War from 1813 to 1814 and participated in the well-known Battle of the Horseshoe on March 27, 1814, he continued his work on his unique alphabet despite the fact that even tribal leaders deemed his dream a work of evil. After a hunting accident which left him permanently disabled, Sequoya was able to devote more time to his studies and alphabetical work. Overtime, his efforts must have gained him some respect; the fact that the name "George Guess, was appended to a treaty of 1816, indicates that he was already of some prominence in the Indian Nation, even before the perfection of his great invention."

In 1821, after repeated attempts and failures, Sequoya submitted his phonetic system of language—an 85-character alphabet, "to a public test by the leading men of the Nation." Their own talking leaf "was soon recognized as an invaluable invention for the elevation of the tribe, and within a few months thousands of hitherto illiterate Cherokee were able to read and write their own language, teaching each other in the cabins and along the roadside." The book-smart Indian had borrowed many of his symbols from an English grammar book, and added other "marks" that was necessary to complete the task. Each symbol represented a sound in the Cherokee tongue, which was an Iroquoian language that was spoken in Tennessee, Georgia, and other places in the South; other closely related tongues include the Mohawk, Oneida, and Seneca-Cayuga. The alphabet helped to catapult the Cherokee to a "front rank among native tribes and was destined to have profound influence on their whole future history," as a result.

In 1822 Sequoya traveled west to Arkansas in order "to introduce the new science among those who had emigrated" there. The very next year he returned to Arkansas and, for the first time, put down roots in the West. The success and popularity of the alphabet continued to spread; however, there were "no schoolhouses…built and no teachers hired, but the whole Nation became an academy for the study of the system." And, even though the Christian missionaries that at first judged and opposed Sequoya's new invention because of its Native American origin,

TIMELESS STORIES OF THE WEST

suddenly had a change of heart and saw it as a means for their own advantage to spread their doctrines. Before long, in 1824, John Arch (Atsi), a young Christian native convert, had made the first Bible translation ever given to the Cherokee—a sampling of the Gospel of St. John. The very next year, a mixed-blood Christian preacher, David Brown, unveiled a complete version of the New Testament using Sequoya's syllabary.

Sequoya's alphabet also spawned the nation's first American Indian newspaper: the *Cherokee Phoenix*. The paper was printed in both Cherokee and English at New Echota, Georgia, on February 21, 1828; Elias Boudinot became the editor. "The office was a log house. The hand press and [custom-made] types, after having been shipped by water from Boston, were transported two hundred miles [overland] by wagon...Such was the beginning of journalism in the Cherokee nation."

The hope was that at long last, having "a constitution and national press, a well-developed system of industries and home education, and a government administered by educated Christian men, the Cherokee were now justly entitled to be considered a civilized people." But trials and troubles for Native Americans continued to plague them as their forced removals confronted them—the loss of their homelands and the sacred burial grounds of their ancestors—regardless of their Christian and civilized status.

About their relocation to the West, John Ross, Cherokee leader of the Ross Party, addressed Congress on May 17, 1834, and had this to say: "Without affecting to pass judgment on the controversy, the writer thinks this memorial well deserving of reproduction here as evidencing the devoted and pathetic attachment with which the Cherokee clung to the land of their fathers, and, remembering the wrongs and humiliations of the past, refused to be convinced that justice, prosperity, and happiness awaited them beyond the Mississippi." Over 4,000 Cherokees would perish on what became known as their "Trail of Tears" to the West.

Sequoya, the inventor and teacher, relocated to Indian Territory (Oklahoma) in 1829; he made his cabin-home a few miles northeast of present-day Sallisaw, Oklahoma. He died in 1843 searching for a legendary tribe of Cherokees that were suppose to be in Mexico. His life-long contributions so impressed the nation that it named the Sequoia National Park and the giant Sequoia trees of California in his honor. Despite the many obstacles that stood in the way of their pursuit of happiness, Sequoya's gift to his people may have been best summoned up in this way: "The invention of the alphabet had an immediate and wonderful effect on Cherokee development."

Bibliography

Chronicle of America, Chronicle Publications, Mount Kisco, New York, 1989.

Faragher, John Mack, *Out of Many: A History of the American People*, Prentice Hall, Upper Saddle River, New Jersey, 1994.

Funk & Wagnall New Encyclopedia, Funk & Wagnall, Inc., New York, 1979.

Mooney, James, *Myths of the Cherokee*, Nineteenth Annual Report of the Bureau of American Ethnology to the Secretary of the Smithsonian Institution, 1900.

Royce, *Cherokee Nation*, Fifth Annual Report of the Bureau of Ethnology, 1888.

Black Hills Betrayal and the Last Stand

GREED AND broken promises and treaties with Native Americans was never more apparent than when considering the gold rush in the Black Hills region of Dakota Territory. The sacred Black Hills of the Lakota Sioux, with its sparkling creeks and streams, piney hills, rolling scenic valleys, and fertile farmland, possessed even more—an abundance of mineral deposits. The value of these precious things was too tempting for many whites, and they were more than willing to overlook boundaries and ownership to trespass for the opportunity to become rich at the expense of their uncivilized neighbors.

The Sioux, to some degree, foolishly trusted in the hollow promises that were made to them by the United States government—and, as a result, the ground was ripe-for-the-taking and wide-open for an unbeknownst invasion. In most cases the Native Americans were outmanned and outgunned, and "Manifest Destiny"—the faith-based belief that God had given all of North America to the whites, was their "free pass" to kill, decimate, conquer, and bask in the glory and bounty of the Black Hills. The increasing appearance of the whites and their continued attempt to snatch up all the best lands in the nation would, eventually, have some dire consequences; adding to that, the killing off of the American bison to near extinction—about 4 million slaughtered by white buffalo hunters in order to starve the Indians who depended upon the animal for meat and other things, began to fight back.

TIMELESS STORIES OF THE WEST

Above: Indians attacking a white settlement.
Below: Bison crossing a railroad track on the Great Plains.

(From: *History of Our Country*, Reuben Post Halleck,
American Book Company, 1923.)

Black Hills Betrayal and the Last Stand

In 1868 a treaty was signed at Fort Laramie in the heart of Sioux country (present-day Wyoming) which blocked non-governmental incursions into the Black Hills. When the U.S. government failed to protect the Indian lands from encroachment, the tribal chiefs, which also included Red Cloud of the Tetons, were left with the less peaceful alternative of enforcing the treaty themselves. Before long, an all out war was underway between miners and Native Americans.

In the early part of 1874, General Philip Sheridan made a recommendation to the U.S. government that a military base needed to be created in the Black Hills to deal with all of the problems that were taking place. As a result, Gen. Sheridan ordered Lieutenant Colonel George Armstrong Custer, along with a regiment of 1,000 soldiers, almost 2,000 mules and horses, a number of Gatlin guns, and over 100 wagons, to set out from Fort Abraham Lincoln which was located across the Missouri River from Bismarck, North Dakota, in July 1874, to thoroughly explore and reconnoiter the Black Hills country. The plan was to seek out and verify its natural resources and to find a suitable place for an army post (Fort Meade was established in 1878).

After Colonel Custer had scouted for two months and sent back word confirming an abundance of gold, a loud cry rose up from all over the country to open up the Black Hills for settlement and robust prospecting—by force if need be. The planned military post could help to protect all of the Argonauts headed for the new gold fields in the coveted area. To complete the desecration, the Northern Pacific Railroad was building a route through, as well, and it also depended upon military oversight.

As early as 1857, Moses and Fred Manuel had wandered into the Black Hills in search of gold. The Manuel brothers founded the Homestake Mine near the hamlet of Lead and proceeded to work it; however, they sold the Homestake Mining Company to George Hearst in the spring of 1877. Illegal mining districts were made at French Creek, Whitewood Gulch, and Black Tail Gulch.

The government tried to offer money to the Sioux for their lands, but they refused the offer. In order to apply pressure and force them to sell, the U.S. army threatened to cut-off their winter supplies and provisions, the Sioux relented and thousands of miners flowed into the northern Black Hills region with pick-ax and shovel in hand—even before the agreement was finalized. In retaliation for all of the intrusions into the Black Hills, the Sioux and Cheyenne began to leave their designated areas—reservations, and do a little intruding of their own upon white lands. This, of course, was all the reason the army needed to make war on the defiant, hostile Indians. This seemed to be an easy solution to all of their gold-greedy, nation-grabbing problems.

Col. George Armstrong Custer who was born in Rumley, Ohio, and schooled at West Point Military Academy, and had served in the American Civil War as a general in battles like Bull Run, Gettysburg, in the Shenandoah Valley, and in General Ulysses S. Grant's final campaigns, was made commander of the 7th Cavalry. Col. Custer was ordered to the Dakota Territory for the purpose of protecting railroad surveyors and prospectors in the region. For three years Custer and his force fought Sioux warriors under chiefs Sitting Bull, Crazy Horse, and Rain-in-the-Face until June 25, 1876, when he waged his last Indian fight at the Battle of the Little Bighorn.

The Sioux camp was located near the Bighorn and Little Bighorn rivers in what is now present-day Montana. Sitting Bull's warrior-force of hostile tribes in the territory numbered between 12,000 to 15,000, consisting of the Uncpapa tribe under Gall, Crow King, and Black Moon; the Sans Arcs under Spotted Eagle; the Minneconjoux under the leadership of Hump; the Brule; the Northern Cheyenne under White Bull, Two Moons, and Little Horse; and finally, the Ogallala under Crazy Horse, Big Road, and Low Dog. It is said that Sitting Bull was making "medicine" and did not participate personally in the massacre but declared victory because of the power of his necromancy (conjuring up the spirits of their ancestors to influence the outcome of the battle).

The army's regiment was divided into three battalions which consisted of Col. Custer (part of the forces of General Alfred Howe Terry), Major M.A. Reno, and Captain F.W. Benteen; Captain T.M. McDougall was left to guard the pack-train. Gen. Custer had at his personal command 264 men to attack what he mistakenly believed was a small band of Sioux; however, he was in reality surrounded

Black Hills Betrayal and the Last Stand

by about 2,500 to 4,000 of Sitting Bull's and Crazy Horse's wild-for-blood, angry braves. As Custer's force neared the river's mouth he could hear the sounds of gunfire, and as was his battlefield custom to do, he rode towards the sound of it and encountered the enemy in force. In the hilly terrain on the east bank of the Little Bighorn, Custer and his men were quickly overrun and under attack. In a last ditch effort to hold out against the enemy, the troopers shot their faithful horses to use as a breastworks to shield themselves from the deadly onslaught of the whizzing lead and screaming arrows. It didn't take long before Col. Custer and his entire personal command and two flanking columns to be wiped-out. Custer's body was later discovered on the pinnacle of a hill with the 7th Cavalry flag still flapping above him; ironically, however, the only living and breathing survivor was Captain Myles Keogh's horse, Comanche.

One historian made this comparison: "Tennyson's poem, *The Charge of the Light Brigade*, tells of English heroes. Custer's fight was more heroic, for not one 'rode back.'"

After the short-lived, bloody conflict, some of the Indian warriors took the liberty of stripping the soldiers and mutilating those in uniform. The fact that Custer failed to join up with Gen. Terry at the confluence of the Bighorn and Little Bighorn rivers and chose instead to attack at once with his smaller force, may have been his fatal mistake. Whether or not his being at the bottom of his West Point class in 1861 had anything to do with the deadly outcome, might only be a matter of interpretation or opinion. The Battle of the Little Bighorn (or the Battle of the Greasy Grass according to Native Americans), will forever be remembered as a time when Manifest Destiny and God's will was clouded by Custer's Last Stand. As for the Black Hills gold rush, the Homestake Mine, for instance, stayed in continual operation for 126 years and finally ceased in 2002.

The program of forced assimilation and Christianization was considered threatened by the Ghost Dance cult; as a result, the U.S. army, including some of Custer's 7th Cavalry, pursued the Indians to Wounded Knee Creek where, on December 29, 1890, between 153 to 300 were massacred. The Sioux surrendered on January 15, 1891.

Bibliography

Barnard, Edward, S., *Story of the Great American West*, The Reader's Digest Association, Inc., Pleasantville, New York, 1977.

Crain, Mary Beth, *Haunted U.S. Battlefields: Ghosts, Hauntings, and Eerie Events from America's Fields of Honor*, Globe Pequot Press, Guilford, Connecticut, 2008.

Funk & Wagnalls New Encyclopedia, Funk & Wagnalls, Inc., New York, 1979.

Goldfield, David, *The American Journey: A History of the United States*, Prentice Hall, Upper Saddle River, New Jersey, 1998.

Halleck, Reuben Post, *History of Our Country*, American Book Company, 1923.

Hanson, Joseph Mills, *The Conquest of the Missouri: The Story of the Life and Exploits of Captain Grant Marsh*, A.C. McClurg, Chicago, Illinois, 1909. (Reprint: Stackpole Books, 2003.)

Legrand, Jacques, *Chronicle of America*, Chronicle Publications, Inc., Mount Kisco, New York, 1989.

Mangum, Neil C., *The Little Bighorn Campaign*, Volume 23, Issue 2, Blue and Gray Magazine, 2006.

Mayo, Matthew P., *Sourdoughs, Claim Jumpers & Dry Gulchers: Fifty of the Grittiest Moments in the History of Frontier Prospecting*, TwoDot, Globe Pequot Press, Guilford, Connecticut, 2012.

Muzzey, David Saville, *The United States of America: II From the Civil War*, Ginn and Company, Boston, 1924.

John Colter: Missouri's Legendary Mountain Man

THE BUSTLING success of St. Louis, Missouri, was the result of no coincidence, being located at the confluence of the Missouri and Mississippi rivers in America's heartland. These artery-highways—before and during the steamboat era, made this "gateway" city a natural base to Western exploration and commercial conquest. Even before this time, Native Americans had also utilized the vantage ground of the same area for their own purpose and livelihoods.

First inhabited by the "Mississippi people," a large population of mound builders that left their handiwork as a sign of their approval of the area, would go on to build over twenty earthen mounds; however, the mounds that were constructed on the Missouri side of the Mississippi River were later destroyed by settlers making room for the city's expansion.

It all began for the whites in 1763 when a French merchant in New Orleans, Louisiana, Pierre Laclede and his 14-year-old son, Auguste Chouteau, headed north with the plan of trading with Native Americans that lived along the Missouri and Mississippi rivers. The dangers involved with such a venture was taken up by author Mark Twain in his book *Life on the Mississippi*, when he wrote about some of the river Indians on the Missouri, warning about "that savage river…descending from its mad career through a vast unknown of barbarism.…"

TIMELESS STORIES OF THE WEST

A typical wharf lined with steamboats.
(From: *Old Times on the Upper Mississippi*, George Byron Merrick,
Arthur C. Clark Company, 1909.)

John Colter

When Laclede discovered a commanding site overlooking the confluence of the two great rivers—some 30-feet above the water's edge, he decided that he had found the spot where he would raise his trading post. The following year while Laclede was absent, he left young Auguste in charge with the man-size task of clearing the land and constructing the post's first buildings. With the help of about thirty others, including some Missouri Indians, they set about to build several log houses and a stone headquarters. Laclede eventually dubbed the new, Old World-style settlement, St. Louis, in honor of France's King Louis IX; a patron saint of King Louis XV. Auguste Chouteau went on to help St. Louis flourish in the fur business, trading with Native Americans and representing the United States to make treaties with them.

Overtime the city grew and prospered as it championed the Western trade. The landing and wharf for steamboats served as a "springboard" for men, goods and supplies headed to and from the beaver country in the West. The busy St. Louis Waterfront filled up with taverns, grogshops, and barrooms to cater to the many needs of the mountain men, river-boatmen, wagon masters, and all types of human contributors. In this environment they took pleasure and the freedom to socialize, gamble, drink, and make plans for "Westering"—or, reminisce about the time they had already spent in the frontier. For some, they splurged until they were penniless and were forced to pull themselves together and head back for another year of trapping in the dangerous and, oftentimes, perilous West.

About the steamboat era, Mark Twain recalled from his days as a steamboat captain how it affected a town and its people when the boats would arrive at a town's landing, writing such things as: "S-t-e-a-m-boat a-comin'!...in a twinkling the dead town is alive and moving. Drays, carts, men, boys, all go hurrying from many quarters to a common centre, the wharf. Assembled there, the people fasten their eyes upon the coming boat as upon a wonder they are seeing for the first time. And the boat *is* rather a handsome sight, too...Ten minutes later the steamer is under way again...after ten more minutes the town is dead again, and the town drunkard asleep by the skids once more." Twain often reminisced about those days and took it with him throughout his life.

TIMELESS STORIES OF THE WEST

One legendary hunter, trapper, and explorer, was John Colter, who was born in Virginia sometime between 1770 and 1775. Colter grew up there and, reportedly, served as an Indian fighter west of the Allegany Mountains before joining Meriwether Lewis and William Clark's Corps of Discovery in the spring of 1804—to explore the newly acquired Louisiana Purchase (1803) which suddenly doubled the size of the United States. At first, Private Colter's duties for the historic expedition was as an oarsman under Sergeant Ordway; however, his impressive skills as a hunter providing sustenance for the party soon put him in the woods and not at the paddle. Another member of the expedition that ranks high and deserves mention is Sacajewea, or "Bird Woman"—the only female member of the group. The young Native American Shoshone teenager, on one occasion, is credited for saving the life of Captain John Smith. She was faithful to Lewis and Clark and their mission and rivals Pocahontas as a heroine of American history.

After two difficult years as a productive member of the Lewis and Clark expedition, while on their way back to St. Louis on August 15, 1806, Colter and the homeward bound explorers encountered Joseph Dickson and Forrest Hancock who were on their way out West to trap beaver. As a result, they persuaded Colter to accompany them—he was more than willing. Colter was so "taken" by the "shining mountains" he had left behind, that he reportedly commented that he would be bored in St. Louis and so he joined Dickson and Hancock. In *The Journals of Lewis and Clark* about their parting of ways, it is recorded that the famous American explorers wished Colter well and shared some supplies with him—assorted articles, black powder, and lead.

Colter spent only one season with his new companions trapping beaver and wintering in a make-shift lean-to shelter. When spring finally arrived, he once again headed downstream in his canoe bound for St. Louis and civilization. Along the way, however, same as before, Colter was approached by a man named Manuel Lisa who was in need of a counselor and guide in the West to help him build a trading post and fort. Colter agreed to Lisa's proposition and went on to help establish his post on the Bighorn River where it emptied into the Yellowstone River. In the winter of 1807-1808, Colter

John Colter

traveled solo along the eastern side of the Absaroka Range, the Wind River Valley, through the Continental Divide at Union Pass, down the Pacific slope and on to the Snake River and the Teton branch of the Rocky Mountains. His winter excursion brought him to his most significant discovery along the Bighorn River to Stinking Water Basin where he was amazed by yellow-stone formations, thermal, volcanic activity of hot springs, erupting geysers, boiling mud-holes, and other natural wonders which fueled his imagination; his enthusiastic reports to the unbelieving, skeptical public later became known as "Colter's Hell." After leaving Yellowstone, he returned to Lisa's post and fort to share the news with them of what he had discovered.

A few months later, Colter was out trapping with a companion named John Potts near the Jefferson Fork of the Upper Missouri River Valley when they were suddenly surrounded by about 500 Blackfeet Indians. Such dangers were described by Mark Twain when he wrote that: "...river Indians were ferocious and pitiless as the river demon, and destroyed all comers without waiting for provocation...."

Poor Potts was riddled with arrows and hacked to pieces. As for Colter, his fate was more sporting—he was given the chance to run for his life. Hundreds of whooping Indian braves gave chase, but Colter was up for the task. He ran on and on but was eventually overtaken by one spear-welding brave; Colter managed to somehow kill him with his own spear. He pressed on more than two hundred long miles back to the safety of Lisa's fort—bloodied and exhausted. After recuperating from the ordeal he returned to his rugged, mountain man lifestyle for about two more years—revenge-killing Blackfeet whenever the opportunity presented itself.

Colter would call it quits in 1810 following another narrow escape with the angry Blackfeet; however, several in his party were deprived of life. This time his eagerness to rejoin civilization and return to St. Louis was heightened and made clear by the fact that he paddled and oared his canoe about 2,000 miles and reached his destination in only about one month.

Unlike Lewis and Clark who kept journals, Colter's time in the frontier did not gain him the same notoriety. And even worse, his wild, persistent tales of Yellowstone seemed more like nightmarish fantasies to the close-minded public.

John Colter went on to settle along the banks of the Missouri River near the mouth of Boeuf Creek about three miles east of present-day New Haven, Missouri. However, his time was short-lived; he died on May 7, 1812, and was buried on a bluff overlooking the river that he had so often traveled. In 1988 a memorial stone with signage was erected three miles east of New Haven, which reads: "Born in Virginia between 1770-75. A member of the Lewis and Clark expedition and the discoverer of Yellowstone Park and Colter's Hell.

"Over a period of only seven years, with his awesome solitary journeys and spectacular escapes from Indians, he became a legend among hunters and trappers while he was still in the mountains.

"In 1810 he left the mountains and settled here in New Port, where only three years later he died from jaundice."

The era that inspired men like John Colter to risk it all for the sake of discovery and opportunity, is now only a bright, glimmering memory of American history. Facing unforgiving elements, walking backwards in order to better recognize the landscape for their return trip, hostile Indians, disease, starvation, bear attacks, injury, infections, and all manner of danger in the untamed West, was the price they paid for that fading but glorious frontier past.

John Colter

Chronology

1770-1775—John Colter is born in Virginia.

1803—The Louisiana Purchase doubles the size of the United States.

1804—Colter joins Meriwether Lewis and William Clark on their Corps of Discovery.

August 15, 1806—Colter leaves Lewis and Clark and heads back West with Joseph Dickson and Forrest Hancock.

1807—Colter heads back towards St. Louis, Missouri, and encounters Manuel Lisa and once again heads back West.

1807-1808—Colter takes a solo tour of the West and discovers Yellowstone.

1810—Colter calls it quits and returns to Missouri.

May 7, 1812—John Colter dies of jaundice and is buried about three miles east of New Haven, Missouri.

Bibliography

DeVoto, Bernard, *The Journals of Lewis and Clark*, Houghton Mifflin Company, Boston, 1953.

Dorsey, Florence L., *Master of the Mississippi: Henry Shreve and the Conquest of the Mississippi*, Literary Classics, Inc., New York, 1941.

Gilbert, Bil, *The Old West: The Trailblazers*, Time-Life Books, Alexandria, Virginia, 1973.

Halleck, Rueben Post, *History of Our Country*, American Book Company, New York, 1936.

Harris, Bill, *How the West was Won: The Mountain Men*, Skyhorse Publishing, New York, N.Y., 2011.

Jackson, Rex T., *St. Louis and the 14-Year-Old Boy, Auguste Chouteau, Who Founded It*, Vol. 9, No. 1, The Ozarks Reader Magazine, Neosho, Missouri, 2012.

Menke, David, *Missouri's Mountain Man Explorer: John Colter*, Vol. 50, No. 4, The Ozarks Mountaineer, Kirbyville, Missouri, 2002.

Twain, Mark, *Life on the Mississippi*, Hartford: American Publishing Company, 1883.

Bullies, Wovoka, and the Massacre at Wounded Knee Creek

IN THE EARLY 1880s, white activists and Christian Protestants pressured the Bureau of Indian Affairs to establish a criminal code which would deny Native Americans the freedom to practice their religion. In 1884 their dream came true and a code was enforced—Indian ceremonies, like the Sun Dance of the Plains Indians, were broken up and their necessary supplies and rations were withheld to force compliance and conformity.

In *The American Journey: A History of the United States* it tells about Christian missionaries who worked to beget reluctant Indian converts. The book offers a quote from a member of the Crow tribe who complained that there were just too many versions of the white man's faith and, for the most part, they only used them for their own worldly gain.

Always searching for new ways to make a profit at the expense of the Indians, constant pressure on the United States Congress finally gave birth to the Dawes Severalty Bill in 1887; the bill was sponsored by Massachusetts Senator Henry L. Dawes and a little inspiration from a book published in 1881 by Helen H. Jackson, titled *A Century of Dishonor*. In the book it talks about the United States government and how it always broke its promises with Native Americans.

Concerning the Dawes Act, it bestowed "...one hundred and

sixty acres of land and United States citizenship upon heads of Indian families who should renounce their tribal allegiance. The purpose of this act was not alone to break up the Indian tribes, whose resentment at having their reservations continually pushed westward by the advancing frontier of [white] settlement had led to conflicts costing the government millions of dollars since the [American] Civil War, but also to satisfy the land hunger of the Western emigrants."

The United States government and Christian organizations utilized education as a weapon against long-held Native American beliefs and traditions. Indian children were muscled away and separated from their families and tribes and isolated at boarding schools where they were brainwashed and forced to speak only in the English tongue—while whites could learn and speak any tongue they desired; of course, the children were also forced to attend church services. While Christians enjoyed their freedom of religion guaranteed by the United States Constitution, Indians learned that others were not, which further confused them. The old Indian ways were doomed—they were outmanned, outgunned, and at the mercy of rich and powerful whites who used politics and pulpits to dominate, decimate, and destroy them. Their last chance at religious freedom, however, came in the late 1880s by way of a Paiute (Piute) healer-shaman named Wovoka; but the movement would only end in death and tragedy.

Wovoka, also known as Jack Wilson, was born around 1856 in present-day Mineral County, Nevada; he would live until 1932. At one time, Wovoka had worked for a rancher and had taken on his Anglo name. As a descendant of Paiute healers, Wovoka was reported to have suffered from fever and delirium in 1888—and, as a result, claimed to have had, at this time, a personal encounter with the Great Spirit: Standing in the presence of the Almighty he was told the buffalo would return to roam the Great Plains; that all of the ancestral tribesmen and Native Americans would once more inhabit the lands; and that all the whites and their works would eventually disappear. God told Wovoka to go to his people and tell them to love one another, work hard, and live in peace, and in the end they would be embraced in the afterlife. Finally, he was told to teach the people a dance, and if it was performed properly, they would be able to get a glimpse of what possible wonders awaited them.

Wovoka's trance reportedly lasted for three days, and many of his people thought that he was dead and they wanted to prepare a final resting place for him; however, Wovoka's wife, Mary, convinced them otherwise. To bring him out of his trance they tried hot flames on his feet and threw water on him to get a reaction, but nothing seemed to work. Finally, on the third day he awoke and called a meeting at the ceremonial grounds where he related his divine message to them.

The pro-Indian prophesies of the holy man spread like wildfire across the western reservations, and many believed. By 1890 it had reached the Sioux people in the Dakotas—into the Pine Ridge, Standing Rock, Cheyenne River, and Rosebud Reservations. The people learned the "Spirit Dance" ritual and some called it the "Dance of the Circle," but the whites dubbed it: the "Ghost Dance." The popularity of the dance, though, was seen as a threat to the government's program of assimilation and Christianization. The Indian dancers also had fears that their new-found religion would be banned and that they would be attacked and murdered; so they created and dawned special "ghost shirts" which had painted-on symbols which they believed would protect them from the bullets of the white man's many guns. They danced and chanted for days and nights and had visions and sweet dreams of good hunting grounds; and of the old days before the whites came. They danced and danced in peace, hope, and happiness, until they were almost exhausted.

Then, everything changed in a "New York minute" when their joy was suddenly crushed and turned into despair—thousands of federal troops were sent-in to the Pine Ridge and Rosebud Agencies to instill fear and send a message that the Ghost Dance would not be tolerated. It was a sad American story of "church and state" working together in harmony to quell the threat of this Native American communal revival. They were being forced to give up their faith and individuality and conform—or face the consequences. Few were brave enough to speak out for them; however, there was one white man, Vallentine McGillycuddy, a former Indian agent who was sent in by the government to make an evaluation of the situation, who reported back saying that Christians, like the Seventh-Day Adventists, sported robes and gathered together to prepare for the Advent of Christ, so he cautioned that Native Americans should have the same such privileges and rights. McGillycuddy's report was ignored and today the Ghost Dance religion is only a forgotten footnote in American history. The problems facing the Native Americans continued, however, and quickly went from bad to worse at a place called Wounded Knee Creek in the Pine Ridge Reservation, South Dakota.

On December 15, 1890, under the orders of Major General Nelson A. Miles, Indian Agent James McLaughlin of the Standing Rock Agency, along with some Sioux Indian police, arrested Chief Sitting Bull and, as a result, a confrontation erupted which caused the death of six Indian police, six Hunkpapa Sioux Indians, and Sitting Bull. The death of the popular chief did not set well with the tribes. About 400 of Sitting Bull's loyal Hunkpapas headed south toward the Cheyenne River Indian Reservation where the army, with the help of Chief Hump of the Miniconjou tribe, convinced most of Sitting Bull's braves to surrender at Fort Bennett; however, about 38 of them headed west and joined Chief Big Foot at his village on the Cheyenne River. Lieutenant Colonel Edwin V. Sumner had orders to arrest Big Foot and had the village under close scrutiny and surveillance. Knowing that this was the case, on December 23, 1890, Chief Big Foot decided to lead his people and Sitting Bull's Hunkpapas, numbering a total of about 350 souls, to the Pine Ridge Indian Reservation with the hopes of finding safety. After waiting for the cover of darkness they headed south through the rugged "Badlands" of South Dakota.

By December 28, 1890, the United States 7th Cavalry, ironically, Lieutenant Colonel George Armstrong Custer's old command, had caught up to the fleeing band of renegade Indians and ordered them to surrender. Big Foot reluctantly obeyed and they received a military escort to a place called Wounded Knee Creek, which is about 70 miles southeast of Rapid City, South Dakota, where they made camp. The former Ghost Dancers were surrounded and under siege by about 500 well-armed (primed for some Little Bighorn

Bullies, Wovoka, and the Massacre at Wounded Knee Creek

"pay-back") soldiers, which included four Hotchkiss machine guns. (The Hotchkiss revolving cannon was the brainchild of Benjamin Berkeley Hotchkiss; the first gun fired one-pound shells, but later they were made to fire six-pounders.)

On the frigid, cold winter morning of December 29, 1890, Colonel James Forsyth and his command entered Big Foot's camp and demanded their weapons. While tensions ran high, and the Indians lingered to disarm, the soldiers began to hastily search the camp and the people—and, in so doing, one young Indian brave, Black Coyote, discharged his weapon. As a result, all hell broke loose and, in seconds, between 153 and 300 Indian men, women, and children were massacred—no match for the army's overwhelming firepower; 25 soldiers were also killed—some, reportedly, by "friendly" crossfire.

Word traveled fast of the bloody massacre and of the extremes the whites would stoop to achieve their goals, and on January 15, 1891, the Sioux and others surrendered and gave up on their Ghost Dance religion and any hope of freedom. Their future was planned by bullies and conquerors, while the dreams and visions of Wovoka eluded them. The Great Plains would have to go on without the thunderous sounds of the buffalo; and the hunting, gathering, equestrian lifestyle, which centered on the horse they had dubbed the "holy dog," would have to remain forever in the past with their ancestors.

TIMELESS STORIES OF THE WEST

"As I slept, I dreamed a dream."

Author-preacher John Bunyan was born in Elstow, England, near Bedfordshire in 1628; he died in 1688. Bunyan's prose, Christian, allegory tale became one of the most treasured books in the English language–next to the Bible.

(Illustration from: *The Pilgrim's Progress from This World to That Which Is to Come*, John Bunyan, The John C. Winston Company, 1896.)

Bibliography

Barnard, Edward S., *Story of the Great American West*, The Reader's Digest Association, Inc., Pleasantville, New York, 1977.

Bunyan, John, *Bunyan's Pilgrim's Progress: In Words of One Syllable*, The John C. Winston Company, 1896.

Crain, Mary Beth, *Haunted U.S. Battlefields: Ghosts, Hauntings, and Eerie Events from America's Fields of Honor*, Globe Pequot Press, Guilford, Connecticut, 2008.

Golay, Michael, and Bowman, John S., *North American Exploration*, Castle Books, 2006.

Goldfield, David, *The American Journey: A History of the United States*, Prentice Hall, Upper Saddle River, New Jersey, 1998.

Legrand, Jacques, *Chronicle of America*, Chronicle Publications, Inc., Mount Kisco, New York, 1989.

Muzzey, David Saville, *The United States of America: II From the Civil War*, Ginn and Company, Boston, 1924.

John Louis O'Sullivan and the "Manifest Destiny" Expansion Crusade

THE IDEA of western expansion has tempted and caused continental avarice in America for centuries. The notion that a civilized society should have the right to make a conquest of the West on account of "Providence" is a lingering mindset. Religious beliefs, national pride, and patriotism, cried out for exploration, colonization, and domination, believing it to be fate and God's will. The cost of western expansion and such thinking caused a number of wars throughout American history.

During the American Revolution, for example, George Rogers Clark, a militia leader from Harrodsburg, Kentucky, was determined to rid the Northwest Territory of the British, loyalists, and hostile Native Americans. With the blessing of Governor Patrick Henry of Virginia, Clark launched a military expedition with a small army of hunters and Indian fighters to surprise and capture Kaskaskia, a British outpost located on the Mississippi River (near East St. Louis, Illinois). On the night of July 4, 1778, the British surrendered at Kaskaskia to Clark's 180 troops.

After this, Clark and his force headed for British-held Vincennes, and during their march they had to pass through some "ice cold water" where Clark, in order to urge his men forward, reported later that: "I viewed their confusion for about one minute, whispered to those near me to do as I did, immediately took some

TIMELESS STORIES OF THE WEST

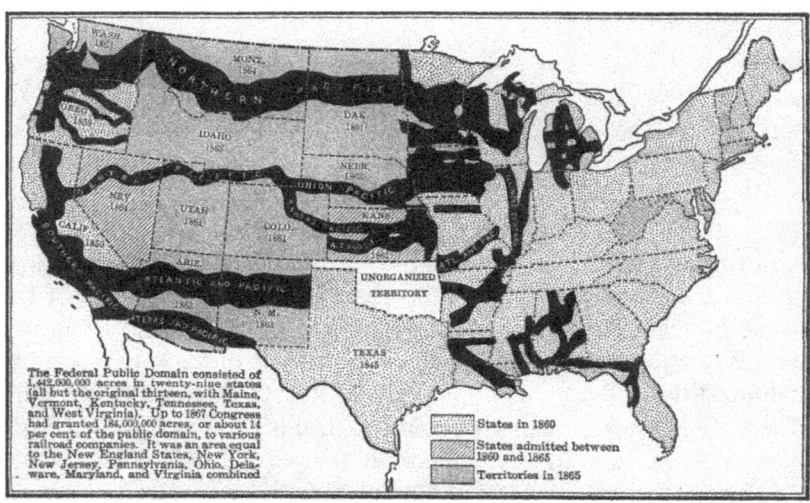

Illustration of the political organization of the West,
and the land grants of the railroads.

(From: *The United States of America: II From the Civil War*,
David S. Muzzey, Ginn and Company, 1924.)

John Louis O'Sullivan

water in my hand, poured on some powder, blacked my face, gave a war whoop, and marched into the water without saying a word. The party gazed and fell in one after another, like a flock of sheep. I ordered those near me to begin a favorite song of theirs. It soon passed through the line and the whole went on cheerfully."

The southwestern Illinois town of Vincennes was completely caught off guard, and the most important British outpost in the Ohio Valley on the Wabash River, under the command of Lieutenant Governor Henry Hamilton, surrendered on February 24, 1779; Hamilton had a "dark" reputation and was dubbed the "hair-buyer" because he was known to have bought scalps from the Indians to encourage the death-toll of his enemies. As a result of Clark's campaign and the war in the West, the states of Ohio, Indiana, Illinois, Michigan, and Wisconsin, were added to the United States which helped clear the way for further conquest across the continent.

Before 1803 and the Louisiana Purchase and Lewis and Clark's expedition, the Mississippi River served as the westernmost boundary of the United States. President Thomas Jefferson's sponsorship of these things went a long way to bring about and further the zest for expansionism; the Louisiana Purchase about doubled the size of the nation.

Not long after that in the 1820s, John Quincy Adams prophesied, in so many words, that the United States was destined by God and nature to some day become the most powerful, populated continent ever assembled under one cooperative human contract. Adams must have foreseen a growing nation.

In 1845 America's evolutionary history was considered by some to be robust nationalism or militarism, with the acquisition of Spanish-held California, Oregon Territory under the British, Russian Alaska, and the annexation of Texas from Mexico; and others. The nation needed to be able to rationalize its insatiable hunger for western expansion, and it needed a catchphrase to believe in, in order to justify land-grabbing. The word-gift came from a man named John Louis O'Sullivan.

John O'Sullivan, a newspaperman and later a diplomat, was born in 1813 and died in 1895, and was best-known for coining the popular catchword "Manifest Destiny," in one of his editorials. O'Sullivan supported the annexation of Texas and wrote about it in the July-August, 1845, edition of the *United States Magazine and Democratic Review*; a magazine he helped to establish. In it he wrote that it was the "Manifest Destiny to overspread the continent" and that the territorial expansion of the nation was ordained by God.

O'Sullivan argued that it was America's God-given right and responsibility to offer democracy to less-developed peoples like the Mexicans and Native Americans—even by force if necessary. Missionary workers and racists combined to conveniently spread their message to others. Christians sought to civilize the Indians, which included the complete destruction of their culture and way of life. Between 1845 and 1848, many thanks to the influential Manifest Destiny watchword, the United States expanded about 70 percent in size and dominated the North American continent. In those three years was "...gained nearly all the land west of the Louisiana Purchase to the Pacific,—the largest addition in our history [so far]. We now had a new coast line of more than a thousand miles on the Pacific." Twenty years after this O'Sullivan's clever phrase was still being utilized to snatch-up Alaska, and before the turn-of-the-century (1900), the acquisition of the Hawaiian Islands and the Spanish territories in the Pacific Ocean were also absorbed into the mix.

O'Sullivan went on to receive an appointment by President Franklin Pierce to serve a four year diplomatic post in Portugal. He eventually returned to the United States early in the 1870s and finally retired in New York.

After the American Civil War in 1865 "...the prevailing high prices, the return of hundreds of thousands of men from the ranks, the renewal of immigration on a large scale, and the government's encouragement of the transMissouri railroads all led to an eager rush for the West...Emigrant and freight trains followed each other in an unbroken stream across the plains...." An 1860s song bragged:

"Of all the mighty nations in the East or in the West
This glorious Yankee nation is the greatest and the best;
We have room for all creation and our banner is unfurled,
Here's a general invitation to the people of the world."

John Louis O'Sullivan

The ongoing expansionist, Christian crusade that sweep across the North American continent and beyond, which obtained a considerable boost from a convenient 19th century catchphrase, gave its followers all the justification they needed to satisfy their land-hungry ambitions. The results are the current boundaries that divide the United States of America from its neighbors—a rewarding perk of Manifest Destiny.

TIMELESS STORIES OF THE WEST

Bibliography

Athearn, Robert G., *American Heritage New Illustrated History of the United States*, Volume 6, *The Frontier*, Fawcett Publications, Inc., One Astor Plaza, New York, N.Y., 1963.

Faragher, John Mack, *Out of Many: A History of the American People*, Prentice Hall, Upper Saddle River, New Jersey, 1994.

Golay, Michael, and Bowman, John S., *North American Exploration*, Castle Books, 2006.

Guitteau, William Backus, *The History of the United States*, Houghton Mifflin Company, 1942.

Halleck, Reuben Post, *History of Our Country*, American Book Company, 1923.

Legrand, Jacques, *Chronicle of America*, Chronicle Publications, Inc., Mount Kisco, New York, 1989.

Muzzey, David Saville, *The United States of America: II From the Civil War*, Ginn and Company, 1924.

John Augustus Sutter and the California Gold Rush

THE VAST, wide-open spaces of the American West that Anglos sought and desired was already inhabited by mostly Native Americans and Mexicans. The West promised many things, fertile farmland, woodlands, abundant game, fruit and nuts, fresh water, plant-life, building materials, mineral deposits, and gold, silver, lead, and so on. Christian missionaries and their advocates led the way for hordes of white settlers, which provided the moral high ground to trespass, survey, and settle the land; and when it became necessary, the United States military was called in to lend a helping hand to the Anglo pioneers. The discovery of precious metals and other benefits made the West a magnet for expansion—and, before long, everything changed for America's first inhabitants. On the other hand, history books made icons of early pioneers and raved over their frontier trials and tribulations. One such well-known name in American history that enjoys being a household name is John Sutter and his famous Sutter's Mill; however, what is often overlooked is that much of Sutter's early success was a result of forced Indian labor.

Johann (John) Augustus Sutter was born in Kandern, Baden, Germany, on February 15, 1803. His parents were from Switzerland, which was nearby, so he attended school in Neuchatel and also served in the Swiss army. In 1834 Sutter immigrated to

Illustration of the San Francisco area of California.

John Augustus Sutter

America and traveled west to St. Louis, Missouri, where he remained for a few years until deciding to relocate to the West Coast. He arrived in the Mexican province of California in 1839 and, eventually, obtained permission from the Mexican government to establish a colony in the Sacramento Valley at the confluence of the American and Sacramento Rivers; the colony that Sutter started was known as New Helvetia. The very next year on August 29, 1840, Sutter became a Mexican citizen. In 1841 Sutter bought Fort Ross (Mendocino) with its redwood walls, blockhouses, and church. The fort was established in 1812 by the Russians as a trading post with regular trading between Mission San Rafael and Mission Sonoma—the sale ended the Russian's presence in the region.

Gold was first discovered in California as early as 1842 by Charles Wilkes, a navy man who did surveying and led expeditions which included the West Coast of America. While in the area, Wilkes and his party visited Sutter and found small amounts of gold in the American River. Another report of gold also came in 1842 from a farmer in the Los Angeles area who claimed to have pulled up an onion for his lunch and found gold dust in its roots.

The fort that would become known as Sutter's Fort was constructed on Sutter's 49,000-acre land grant by enslaved Indians which were kept confined in pens and used as forced labor to build the compound. The fort had all the things necessary within its walls for the many emigrants that were migrating into the area. John Bidwell and John Bartleson led the first emigrant train of 34 settlers to California in 1841; Bidwell liked California so well that he stayed and found employment as an agent at Sutter's Fort. Sutter waxed rich from his sizeable landholdings and business ventures and in the summer of 1846 he was able to help John Charles Fremont during the Bear Flag Revolt; the annexation of California was eventually finalized by the Treaty of Guadalupe in 1848.

During the winter of 1846-47 a group of 87 emigrants known as the Donner Party who were heading for California became snowbound in the Sierra Nevada Mountains. After their supplies ran out, in order to stay alive, they stooped to cannibalism—only 48 of the group survived the ordeal. Sutter reportedly offered help and supplies to rescue the historic Donner Party from further tragedy and horror.

In 1847 Sutter and James Wilson Marshall teamed up to build a new sawmill about 50-miles east of Sutter's Fort. Marshall, a New Jersey mechanic who was born in Lambertville in 1810, ventured out in 1828 to the Midwest where he did farming, but by 1845 he had relocated to California where he found work at Sutter's Fort. Marshall's expertise made him a perfect choice to oversee the construction of Sutter's new mill at Coloma, on the south fork of the American River. On January 24, 1848, however, some of the workers that were excavating at the mill-site discovered gold; some sources say that Marshall was the one that spied it while walking along the riverbank. Regardless of who found it the decision was made to keep the find a secret until it could be ascertained as to whether or not it was in fact real gold and not just "fools gold." But as such things go word spread about the discovery, which at first caused little attention but eventually picked-up steam. One of the culprits that piqued the interest of Americans and people from all over the world was a publicity stunt pulled by Sam Brannan in San Francisco.

Samuel ("Sam") Brannan grew up in Ohio and moved to New York in 1842 and converted to Mormonism. In 1846 he led a party of over 200 Mormons by ship to the West Coast. Brannan settled in San Francisco—where, soon after his arrival, he established the first newspaper, the California *Star*. Eventually, he opened a grocery store at Sutter's Fort hoping to benefit monetarily from the many souls headed to the goldfields that were scattered about the countryside. In order to reap its full effect, the wily entrepreneur came up with the brilliant idea of running through the streets of San Francisco crying out: "Gold! Gold on the American River!" The stunt was so odd and unusual for the times that it did what newspapers failed to do—it created frenzy and a stampede of souls that swamped the area and helped to spawn the California Gold Rush. People poured in from many places—Basques, Croats, Chinese, and Australians, to name a few.

Many mining camps were born, with names like Poker Flat, Gouge Eye, Brandy Gulch, Whisky Bar, Hangtown, Placerville, Hell's Delight, Mariposa, and many, many others. Discrimination was rampant, and many Anglos thought that the gold belonged to them and they lashed-out at the Chinese, Mexicans, African Americans, Indians, and others that they deemed to be inferior races. The dream of a homogeneous West appealed to the whites and, in 1850, the California legislature heard their prejudice outcry and passed the Foreign Miners' Tax Law, which levied unfair taxes on non-Anglo people with the hopes of forcing them from the goldfields and out of their sight. The sinful, disgraceful activities didn't stop there; some were murdered, mistreated, and assaulted, in the land of the free.

The California boom also brought another breed of humanoid: gamblers, gun-totting outlaws, and other unscrupulous characters to fill the colorful spectrum. It was reported that about 10,000 Australians (also known as "Aussies") joined the riff-raff and formed a gang of lawbreakers called the "Sydney Ducks" who went about terrorizing the region.

Another incident, for example, involved a woman known as "Pretty Juanita" who became the first person to be lynched during the gold rush of California. At the time, frontier western towns, for the most part, were ruled by grass-root democracy and vigilantes. Her execution was carried out after she was accused and convicted of knife-murder—stabbing a man who she claimed had insulted her in some way. It is said that Juanita bravely laughed and gave a "good-bye" wave before the hangman's noose ended her life.

However, one of the most well-known lawless figures of the era was Joaquin Murrieta, a Latino hero of the people who was said to have been angered by the terrible outrages perpetrated upon his race, which would eventually bring about the name of "Zorro." This character was later glorified and featured in books, magazines, movies, and other places. Reportedly, Murrieta came to California in 1849 from Sonora, Mexico, and suffered from discrimination and abuse in California's pro-Anglo climate. As a result, he put together an outlaw band of kindred spirits. Murrieta's bandits roamed unabated throughout the countryside for a couple of years on a crime spree of murder and thievery; the desperadoes robbed and killed miners, held-up stagecoaches, and rustled livestock. Murrieta claimed that his wife was sexually assaulted and murdered, his half-brother hung, and his mining claim jumped, so he cared little for anything but vigilante justice and revenge. Finally, in 1853 the state legislature decided they had had enough and ordered the capture of Murrieta and his marauding cohorts. On July 25, 1853, the legend was taken by surprise and killed by the California State Rangers while most of his men were either shot or taken into custody.

This is where it gets macabre, the bandit's head was severed and put into a large glass jar filled with alcohol and displayed throughout the state in jailhouses and saloons as a mobile, gruesome reminder. Tales of Robin Hood-like deeds sprang into existence and continued over the years—probably due to the poor treatment and discrimination that flourished during the gold rush era. In the end, the state legislature did little or nothing to punish or quell the sin of racism, which helped to fuel the lingering legend of Murrieta.

Ironically, the gold rush brought about the end of Sutter's success—squatters and prospectors had overrun his property, slaughtered and eaten his livestock, destroyed and utilized his crops, while his mill set silent with no one to operate it. He became penniless and forced into bankruptcy in 1852. Sutter tried for a number of years to get Congress' help in restoring his many losses, but it fell on deaf ears. Finally, though, the state of California gave him a monthly pension of $250. He later relocated to Lititz, Pennsylvania, where he eventually died in poverty on June 20, 1880. At his funeral at the Moravian Brotherhood Cemetery a few famous people were in attendance, which included author Mark Twain and the old pathfinder, General John Charles Fremont who delivered the eulogy.

About James Marshall, his fate was similar to that of John Sutter; he left this world with no silver or gold. Marshall passed on August 10, 1885, and was laid to rest in Coloma, California.

The California Gold Rush made paupers and princes, saints and sinners, and also history. Forty-niners or Argonauts as they were sometimes called—named after the legendary Greek seamen who sailed aboard the *Argo* in search of the Golden Fleece with Jason, came from all over the world to the boomtowns of the West with the dream of wealth and prosperity. Historical facts are not always kind, but the eye-opening lessons they offer can be a rich treasure trove.

James Augustus Sutter

Bibliography

Athearn, Robert G., *American Heritage New Illustrated History of the United States*, Volume 6, *The Frontier*, Fawcett Publications, Inc., One Astor Plaza, New York, N.Y., 1963.

Dungan, Myles, *How the Irish Won the West*, Skyhorse Publishing, New York, N.Y., 2011.

Enss, Chris, *Tales Behind the Tombstones: The Deaths and Burials of the Old West's Most Nefarious Outlaws, Notorious Women, and Celebrated Lawmen*, TwoDot, Guilford, Connecticut, 2007; *Outlaw Tales of California: True Stories of the Golden State's Most Infamous Crooks, Culprits, and Cutthroats*, TwoDot, Guilford, Connecticut, 2013.

Faragher, John Mack, *Out of Many: A History of the American People*, Prentice Hall, Upper Saddle River, New Jersey, 1994.

Funk & Wagnalls New Encyclopedia, Funk & Wagnalls, Inc., New York, 1979.

Golay, Michael, and Bowman, John S., *North American Exploration*, Castle Books, 2006.

Legrand, Jacques, *Chronicle of America*, Chronicle Publications, Inc., Mount Kisco, New York, 1989.

Mayo, Matthew P., *Sourdoughs, Claim Jumpers & Dry Gulchers: Fifty of the Grittiest Moments in the History of Frontier Prospecting*, TwoDot, Guilford, Connecticut, 2012; *Haunted Old West: Phantom Cowboys, Spirit-Filled Saloons, Mystical Camps, and Spectral Indians*, Globe Pequot Press, Guilford, Connecticut, 2012.

Morgan, Robert, *Lions of the West: Heroes and Villains of the Westward Expansion*, Algonquin Books of Chapel Hill, 2011.

Roark, James L., *The American Promise: A History of the United States*, Bedford Books, Boston, 1998.

Turner, George, *Gun Fighters*, L. Baxter Lane Publisher, Amarillo, Texas, 1972.

Bent's Fort: Colorado's Adobe Oasis

THROUGHOUT the American West, no fortification was more important in size and location than Bent's Fort on the north bank of the Arkansas River near the junction of the Purgatoire River a few miles east of present-day La Junta, Colorado. At the time, the north side of the river was the United States boundary with Mexico and formed the southernmost territory of fur trading; the fort also lay at the western end of the St. Louis-Santa Fe Trail and close to the Old Trapper's Trail that meandered from Taos, New Mexico, to Fort Laramie, Wyoming.

Bent's Fort was a bustling, cross-trailed place where Native Americans came to trade, which included the Southern Cheyenne and the Arapaho of buffalo country, the Comanche and Kiowas of the Canadian River region, the Ute and Gros Ventre, and various other tribes of the area; it was also a sanctuary, trading post, and factory for rugged mountain men; and a refuge and oasis for wagon trains headed west in need of rest and supplies—salt, flour, sugar, coffee, tobacco, ammunition, whiskey, clothing, and so on. Seeing the impressive bulwark coming into view in this wild, wooly, and remote environment must have been a welcome sight for sore eyes. This key fur-trading outpost was an important player in America's westward expansion.

In 1833 the Bent brothers, William and Charles, with their

partner, Ceran St. Vrain, formed Bent, St. Vrain & Company and with the help of some Cheyenne in picking out a suitable site—and Mexican labor, they built Bent's Fort (also known as Fort Williams). Constructed of adobe (sun-dried bricks) walls 4-feet thick and 14-feet high, the two-story fort could house a garrison of about 200 men and 300 animals. The east wall of the quadrangular fort measured about 137 feet, the north 178 feet, the west 180 feet, and the south side about 200 feet. There was a double, iron-sheathed entrance gate on the east side, a watchtower with a belfry which had a telescope, and a popular rooftop billiard table, barroom, and drink called Taos Lightning. The fort had almost everything: storehouses, offices, dormitories, a smithy, icehouse, well, "robe press", corral, various sheds, musket towers, artillery, and much more. There were about 150 men working at the fort with various positions.

Kit Carson and Tom Fitzpatrick provided the bastion plenty of wild game to feast upon—mostly, deer, buffalo, and antelope; and Charlotte, a popular black cook of the fort, was heralded for her mouthwatering pancakes and tasty pumpkin pies. America's famous mountain men frequented this frontier oasis for supplies and often gambled away their hard-earned pelts. Wagon trains brought pioneers, prospectors, and many others who were traveling the Santa Fe Trail for one reason or another to find relaxation, medical relief, and supplies. On July 10, 1842, Lieutenant John C. Fremont of the Army Topographical Corps arrived at Bent's Fort during one of his expeditions; the fort was a supplier of horses, mules, and other things for the United States government—for military and exploratory missions into the Western frontier. Lieut. Fremont probably had secret government orders to take California and not break international laws.

When the Mexican War erupted in 1846, William H. Emory, appointed chief engineer for Colonel Stephen Watts Kearny's Army of the West, along with about 300 dragoons, marched out of Bent's Fort on August 2, 1846, on their way to capture Santa Fe, New Mexico; Emory joined the Corps of Topographical Engineers in 1838. After taking Santa Fe, Col. Kearny's Army of the West eventually met up with Kit Carson near Valrerde, New Mexico, and received the news that California had been taken and declared a

Bent's Fort

Photo of Colorado by Seth Nathan Jackson.

republic—independent of Mexico's rule. On June 14, 1846, "a flour sack on which had been painted a star, a bear, and the words 'California Republic...'" was hoisted into the air; however, the "California Bear Flag" was lowered and replaced by the United States flag on July 11, 1846.

Concerning the Mexican cession, the Treaty of Guadalupe Hidalgo, that brought to an end the Mexican War in 1848, "gave to the United States, in addition to the disputed strip between the Nueces and the Rio Grande, (1) California and (2) the territory to the east including what is now Nevada, Utah, most of Arizona and New Mexico, and parts of Wyoming and Colorado. This region contained 529,000 square miles of new territory and ranked next in size to the Louisiana Purchase. The treaty with Mexico extended the southern boundary of Texas to the Rio Grande...The southern boundary of Arizona and New Mexico was completed by the Gadsden purchase (1853) of 30,000 square miles of territory...."

After the United States boundaries had changed, Bent decided to offer the government the opportunity of buying the stronghold, but they declined. As a result, in 1849 he placed charges of black-powder throughout the post and blew it to smithereens and built a new fort 40 miles downriver.

Many forts in the West were constructed in the 19th century for the purpose of protection, exploratory expeditions, war, westward expansion, and so on. By the time the Untied States boundaries were established, the usefulness of the forts began to wane. The coming of the railways and better roads was also a contributing factor to the demise of the Western fort; and law and order also helped to tame the Wild West. Scattered across America, however, travelers can still see, in many cases, ruins and historic sites of the forts that once served such an important role in the building of a nation.

Bibliography

Barnard, Edward S., *Story of the Great American West*, Reader's Digest Association, Inc., Pleasantville, New York, 1977.

Coit, Margaret L., *The Life History of the United States*, Volume 4, *The Sweep Westward*, Time-Life Books, New York, 1963.

Golay, Michael, and Bowman, John S., *North American Exploration*, Castle Books, 2006.

Halleck, Reuben Post, *History of Our Country*, American Book Company, 1923.

Parkman, Francis, *The Oregon Trail: Sketches of Prairie and Rocky-Mountain Life,* Little, Brown, and Company, Boston, 1892.

Famed Custer and the Bloody Washita Massacre

THE UNTAMED WEST was like a candy store just begging to be ravished and ransacked. The problem, however, was that the Native Americans wanted to keep it the way it was—unfettered and pristine. The task of westward expansion and controlling the Indian population on the frontier was an ongoing nightmare for the United States government. The American Indians resented "the invasion of their immemorial hunting-grounds by the steady westward migration of the 'pale faces,' [and so] they ambushed the stagecoaches, tore up rails, threw down telegraph poles, and massacred the inmates of the government posts." To make matters worse, there were dishonest and greedy agents of the Indian Bureau that peddled "whisky and firearms, which made the task of the soldiers who were trying to restrain ambush and massacres almost impossible. The Indian Bureau and the War Department were at loggerheads, each accusing the other of inefficiency and inhumanity...."

In 1867 the commissioner of the Indian Bureau gave his 19th century exaggerated view and opinion of the situation and said that it had "cost the government over $40,000,000 to conduct the campaign of 1865; and that at the present rate of extermination [genocide] it would take twenty-five thousand years, at a cost of $300, 000,000,000, to be rid of the 'red fiends.'"

A reproduction Indian dwelling at the Tsa-La-Gi Historic Site in Tahlequah, Oklahoma.

Famed Custer and the Bloody Washita Massacre

General Philip Henry Sheridan who became the commander of the Southwestern Department, a well-known soldier of the American Civil War (defeating the Confederates at Cedar Creek in October 1864 in the Shenandoah Valley of Virginia and spearheading the conflict at Five Forks south of Petersburg), had a rather low and hateful opinion of the American Indian. Stationed in Kansas in 1866 with General William Tecumseh Sherman, who was his superior officer, Gen. Sheridan and Gen. Sherman decided that the only way to get rid of the Plains Indians and their way of life was to exterminate the buffalo—kill the bison and you kill the Indians was the mindset. On another occasion in January 1869, a Comanche chieftain, Tochoway, came to Fort Cobb, Indian Territory, and approached Gen. Sheridan and told him that he was a good, peaceful Indian; "the only good Indian is a dead Indian" was the general's reply.

In November 1868, Gen. Sheridan ordered Lieutenant Colonel (Brevet Major General) George Armstrong Custer who was at Fort Supply—a fortification recently constructed at the mouth of Wolf Creek on the North Canadian River, to ride out in search of the Cheyenne's winter camp. Colonel Custer and his 800-man 7th Cavalry Regiment, baggage train, and guides, made their way to the Washita River where they discovered the village of Black Kettle (Moke-ta-ra-to). The camp located near present-day Cheyenne, Oklahoma, consisted of about 180 lodges, and not far away up and down the Washita River Valley, unbeknownst to Col. Custer, were about 2,000 braves of the Kiowas, Arapahos, Comanches, Apaches, and others that made up about 1,000 more lodges.

The night was cold and a foot of new-fallen snow had blanketed the region, as if to offer a white, sterile landscape for the horrors to come. Black Kettle had somehow survived the Massacre of Sand Creek in Colorado where Colonel J.M. Chivington, a fanatical Christian preacher and his blood-thirsty mob-army, mercilessly attacked and killed Indian men, women, and children. Once again the old chief had no clue or warning as to what was to come. Black Kettle had recently visited Fort Cobb in an attempt to persuade General W.B. Hazen to guarantee safety for his people, but Black Kettle's talk of peace fell on deaf ears.

TIMELESS STORIES OF THE WEST

On November 26, 1868, Col. Custer, or "Long Hair" as the Indians liked to call him, divided his forces into four detachments, leaving his baggage train near Antelope Hills which was on the Canadian River, and posted his army so that Black Kettle's village was completely surrounded. Custer's men lingered throughout the bitter, winter night until the wee morning hours of November 27, 1868. With the sound of bugles and the regimental band playing the popular song *Garryowen*, the 7th Cavalry charged pell-mell into the sleeping, slumbering Indian camp firing their weapons—as a result, it became a slaughter pen of death.

The foredoomed Cheyenne and Arapahos sprang from their lodges to face the onslaught of crazed troopers bearing down upon them. Many of the people were nearly naked and were helpless; Black Kettle and his wife fell in front of their dwelling place; others ran for the river and died in the icy confines of the blood-stained waters; while the whole camp became littered with a mass of dead and dying bodies strewn throughout the snow-covered grounds which was now turned blood-red; finally, the lodges were burned to the ground and the camp looted. There were trampled children and victims of souvenir-scalping to showcase and spotlight the white man's need for revenge-killing and their relentless pursuit of Manifest Destiny. Some concerned Americans cried foul while others thought that such atrocity was justified—just another hot-button issue to divide the nation.

By the time their fellow Indians who were camped nearby heard the commotion and responded, Col. Custer and his army turned-tail and skedaddled, retreating to safety. Left behind to rot in the snow were over 100 men, women, and children—and over 700 Indian ponies; the 7th Cavalry lost about 20 men in the battle-massacre. One of the soldiers who died that historic day was the grandson of Alexander Hamilton—his name was Captain Lewis M. Hamilton. As for Alexander Hamilton, he was born on January 11, 1757, on the West Indian island of Nevis. He wrote polemic (incendiary) pamphlets which impressed George Washington so much that he became his aide-de-camp. Overtime, Hamilton was elected to the Continental Congress; served in the New York Assembly and was appointed Secretary of the Treasury; served as the Inspector of the

Famed Custer and the Bloody Washita Massacre

Army; practiced law; fought for a national bank and for the Constitution, and other noteworthy things. Alexander Hamilton was eventually killed in a duel with Aaron Burr on July 11, 1804.

Col. Custer's work that day at Washita earned him a great deal of fame as an Indian fighter, which probably helped to lead the way to his participation at the Battle of the Little Bighorn. The Washita Massacre also gained Long Hair about 53 Indian squaws and children who were taken captive; and over a thousand buffalo robes, 500 pounds of lead, black powder, thousands of arrows, bows, rifles, saddles, blankets, and many other things—all in a day's work. In the American East some labeled the United States military cowards who attacked sleeping Indian villages and even stooped to murdering innocent, swaddled babes. Others, however, less concerned about crimes against humanity, felt that Indians deserved to be exterminated—America's own genocidal "holocaust" yet to be properly reckoned with.

Bibliography

Legrand, Jacques, *Chronicle of America*, Chronicle Publications, Inc., Mount Kisco, New York, 1989.

Mangum, Neil C., *The Little Bighorn Campaign*, Volume 23, Issue 2, Blue & Gray Magazine, Columbus, Ohio, 2006.

McReynolds, Edwin C., *Oklahoma: A History of the Sooner State*, University of Oklahoma Press, Norman, 1954.

Muzzey, Davis Saville, *The United States of America: II From the Civil War*, Ginn and Company, Boston, 1924.

Wellman, Paul I., *Death on Horseback: Seventy Years of War for the American West,* J. B. Lippincott Company, New York, 1947.

Nathan Boone: Soldier, Surveyor, and Mountaineer

BEFORE the taming of the American West, there were trailblazers, woodsmen, hunters, trappers, Indian fighters, and mountaineers like Daniel Boone. Boone, an unschooled and illiterate but daring individual, carved out a name for himself in the annals of America's rich and vast lands. His eventful life, now an educational source of study for students of history, was forged beginning in the 18th century when he blazed a path through the Cumberland Gap to eastern Kentucky and went on to build a fort and stockade along the Kentucky River on the site of Boonesboro. The trail leading to the fortification became known as the "Wilderness Road." He faced many dangers and hardships and became a well-known advocate for the settlement of the American wilderness.

By 1799, the old Kentucky rifleman following the call of the wild, left his homeland behind and relocated to land west of the Mississippi River, which at the time was under Spain's control; it became a territory of the United States after the Louisiana Purchase in 1803. Before long, ,most of the Boone family had ventured down the Ohio River in order to reunite with Daniel, following the western side of the Mississippi River north to the French established settlement of St. Louis. The Boones' continued their journey a few more miles west on the north bank of the Missouri River all the way to the Femme Osage Valley near present-day Defiance, Missouri, where they discovered Daniel's small, humble cabin. By 1810, however, the Boones' had constructed a grand, 4-story home.

While the War of 1812 was being waged, Missourians complained about British agents who would supply weapons to hostile Indians and encourage them to use the arms against traders and homesteaders. The Sac and Fox of the Rock River Indian tribe were pro-British and often made raids upon a number of places north of the Missouri River; one site that was targeted was Fort Mason, which was located near Hannibal, Missouri, on the Mississippi River—Mark Twain's future home and haunt. The attacks prompted Governor Benjamin Howard to organize a territorial militia to patrol the region—a group of hardcore frontiersmen that were living along the Missouri River. As a result, Nathan Boone served as a Missouri Ranger, Daniel Boone's youngest son who was born in Kentucky in 1781, and Daniel Morgan Boone, the older of the two sons, also served. Major Daniel Morgan Boone later served in 1814 under General Henry Dodge in western Missouri, helping to protect and serve various early pioneer settlements in that area.

Before Daniel Boone's death in 1820 at the "Daniel Boone Home" in Defiance, his sons were already following in his mountaineering footsteps. The Boones' did farming, hunting, and exploring the Missouri River and eventually discovered salt licks in Howard County. Nathan and Daniel Morgan began to manufacture salt at the site as an income by 1805, and the beaten-down-path from their Defiance home to the salt lick became known as "Booneslick Trail," "Boone's Trace," and "Boone's Lick Road." The pioneering spirit that Nathan inherited from his father served him well throughout his life in Missouri, the Ozark Mountain country, and the American West.

Nathan eventually decided to abandon the salt business for an important career in surveying—which he did, surveying the first road across Missouri. He surveyed some of Missouri's counties, the border between Missouri and Iowa, various other roadways, and also did surveying in other states, including Indian Territory (Oklahoma).

In 1820, Nathan dabbled in politics and became a member of the first constitutional convention in Missouri—but, what he is best remembered for is his longtime military service. In 1833 he served as a captain of the dragoons stationed at Fort Gibson in the Indian Nations. The fort was first established on April 21, 1824, by Colonel Matthew Arbuckle, and was at times referred to as Cantonment Davis and Fort Blunt. It was built to keep a watchful eye on hostile Indians, and also for military and further exploratory expeditions into the West. Nathan spent time there and used Fort Gibson as a base of operations while surveying Creek and Cherokee Indian boundaries. Later, however, the historic fort became useful during the American Civil War (1861-1865).

In 1834, Nathan participated in a five-week expedition during the dog days of summer to negotiate with Native Americans in what is now Kansas and the more remote regions of Indian Territory; it was considered the largest expedition ever made into the Nations. He was eventually promoted to the rank of major in the First Dragoons on February 16, 1847, and was commissioned lieutenant colonel in the Second Dragoons in 1850. His military career ended when he resigned on July 15, 1853.

His pioneering spirit gnawed at him until he surrendered to it in 1837 and moved his family south and west to the less-populated area of Greene County just north of Ash Grove, Missouri. It proved what one historian wrote about such 19th century individuals: "…pioneers began to get restless, feeling themselves a little too crowded, and they began to look out for a place where they could have space to breathe in, and there being only one direction for them, which was still westward towards the setting sun, a few of them packed up their goods and chattels, with their wives and little ones, and set out to find a home further west."

With the help of three sons and two slaves he built a dogtrot-style home using hand-hewn native ash logs. Ceiling hooks in the home's entryway became a place where his daughters did quilting. The log cabin had a fireplace built of sandstone at each end, and the outside walls were eventually plastered and the open dogtrot area was later enclosed.

The Boone homestead consisted of 720 rolling, Ozark acres of prairie and open limestone glades. The wooded areas were made up

Final resting place of Nathan Boone at the Nathan Boone Homestead State Historic Site near Ash Grove, Missouri.

of mostly oak, walnut, and ash; many other species are also common to the region, like hickory, persimmon, dogwood, redbud, elm, sycamore, Osage orange, cherry, and so on. There were about 75-100 hogs, 25-40 sheep and cattle, and about 24 horses kept at any given time on the Boone farm.

Nathan Boone died on his Ash Grove farmstead in 1856—five years before the outbreak of the Civil War. There is a small cemetery there where Nathan and his wife, Olive, rest, along with other family members and acquaintances. A second cemetery nearby contains about 14-16 African Americans, some of which predate the War Between the States; a few of the modest stone markers have names etched upon them—two of which, interestingly enough, reads: Moses Boone and Preston Boone.

As an early pioneer, Nathan Boone's name never achieved the well-known historical status as did his famous father's name which was inducted into the Hall of Fame for Great Americans in 1920 along with author Samuel Clemens (Mark Twain) and James Buchanan Eads—the great American civil engineer; both of Missouri, as well. But considering Nathan's work and noteworthy contributions, his name has been, for the most part, unjustly overlooked as an icon of the West.

Bibliography

Borwick, Jim, and Dufur, Brett, *Forgotten Missourians Who Made History*, Pebble Publishing Company, Columbia, Missouri, 1996.

Eckert, Allan W., *The Frontiersmen: A Narrative*, Little, Brown and Company, Boston, 1967.

Jackson, Rex T., *Notable Persons and Places in Missouri's History*, The Ozarks Reader Magazine, Neosho, Missouri, 2006.

McReynolds, Edwin C., *Missouri: A History of the Crossroads State*, University of Oklahoma Press, Norman, 1962.

Nathan Boone Homestead State Historic Site, Ash Grove, Missouri.

Roberts, Robert B., *Encyclopedia of Historic Forts*, Macmillan Publishing Company, Inc., 1987.

Promontory Point: Iron Trail from Coast to Coast

TAKEN FOR granted is the ease in which travel has been simplified and improved by modern inventions and technologies. Early in the 19th century before trains, planes, and automobiles, travelers to America's West Coast from the East were forced to book passage on ships and steam or sail around the southern tip of South America and Cape Horn; some, however, disembarked at Panama and journeyed across the isthmus—overland, to the Pacific Ocean where they again boarded another seagoing vessel headed north; still others chose to join cross-country wagon trains and make the bone-jarring, four-month, 2,000 mile trip enduring unimaginable hardships and dangers. Considering everything that could happen on a wagon train bound west, one traveler told about how one of the greatest fears was being shot accidentally by a fellow member of their own group, since there were so many weapons on the train.

The ruff and rugged experience became too much for some and they gave up their dreams and turned back. Before long, though, times would eventually change, as one historian wrote in the late 1800s: "If they had been told…that boats would be propelled by steam with ease up the Missouri river, they would have thought that you were crazy…that…the Atlantic and Pacific oceans would be tied together by the iron horse, many hooted at the idea, and some said [it] was crazy.

TIMELESS STORIES OF THE WEST

"But we find [the] prediction more than fulfilled. We see the country checkered with railroads in every direction, and people conversing with ease across the continent, as familiarly and socially as if they were sitting together in their home circle...."

As early as the 1820s, the dream of a railroad in America was being followed and pursued. In 1828 the Chamber of Commerce in Charleston, South Carolina, secured a charter to create a railroad from Charleston to Hamburg, located on the Savannah River across from Augusta, Georgia. The 136-mile rail line was completed in 1833 and was, at the time, the longest one on earth.

Not to be outdone, Massachusetts decided to have their own railroad—and, starting in 1830, three lines were chartered from Boston. From 1830 to 1850 about 3,000 miles of railroad track had been laid; and by 1860 there was already about 30,000 miles of track. The earliest railway tracks, however, were crude and made from wooden beams—or rails, butted end to end and covered with iron straps which were nailed on top.

Some of the first trains were so mistrusted that they carried a horse along as an added measure just in case the engine broke down. In order to help gain the confidence of the public, Peter Cooper, an American manufacturer and philanthropist from New York who designed and assembled the first steam locomotive in America—dubbed the *Tom Thumb*, arranged and ran a seven mile contest on September 18, 1830, against a horse on the Baltimore & Ohio Railroad. The one-horsepower *Tom Thumb*, also known as the "tea kettle on a truck," pulled a carload of passengers in its duel with the horse-drawn car but suffered a mechanical breakdown and lost the historic race. Even though the little steamer had failed to win, it proved that such transportation innovation was possible. *Tom Thumb* went on that same year to successfully travel thirty miles from Baltimore, Maryland, to Ellicott's Mill in about an hour, rounding a four-hundred-foot curve during the trial run without incident.

By 1900 there was about 193,000 miles of track crossing and crisscrossing the nation. Before the turn-of-the-century, the steamboat era had, for the most part, given way to the railroads. About the turn-of-events, author and one-time riverboat pilot, Mark

Promontory Point

Photo of an iron horse taken at Eureka Springs, Arkansas.

Twain, writing about the change, lamented: "Half a dozen sound-asleep steamboats...This was melancholy, this was woeful. The absence of the pervading and jocund steamboatman from the billiard-saloon was explained. His occupation is gone...Half a dozen lifeless steamboats, a mile of empty wharves...Here is desolation, indeed."

One of the most monumental achievements of the 19th century, however, was the completion of the transcontinental railroad. The coast-to-coast line would reduce the cross-country journey of several months to about eight days. The Central Pacific Railroad would start in Sacramento, California, in 1863 and blast through the Sierra Nevada and across the hot, dry desert of Nevada 690 miles to meet their rival company, the Union Pacific Railroad; the Union Pacific worked its way westward from Omaha, Nebraska, 1,086 miles through prairies, mountains, and hostile Indian country to link together with the Central Pacific at Promontory Point, Utah, on May 10, 1869.

Two belching, smoking iron horses the Indians liked to call "thunder wagons," faced-off at Promontory Point—the Central Pacific's Jupiter and the Union Pacific's 119. The president of the Central Pacific, Leland Stanford, positioned between the locomotives, swung a silver hammer to drive home the final spike to wed the nation—a spike made of solid gold. Not as talented as the hard-working Chinese of the Central Pacific or the Irish laborers of the Union Pacific, Stanford missed the mark and failed in his task. As entertaining as it was, the vice president of the Union Pacific, Thomas Durant, decided to give it a shot, but like Stanford, Durant was also unsuccessful. Finally, Grenville Mellen Dodge, the chief engineer of the Union Pacific, raised the commemorative hammer and drove the golden spike tight to the rail and connected America from sea to shining sea. All over the country people celebrated the history-making accomplishment—bells tolled and cannons fired, while Native Americans scornfully eyeballed the steel rails that dared to trespass through their sacred grounds.

The Cheyenne and Sioux saw how the noisy, thunderous locomotives scared the buffaloes and scattered the precious multitudes and disrupted their migration patterns, so they retaliated

Promontory Point

by making attacks and sabotaging the track and derailing the trains. The railroads were instrumental in bringing to an end the Indian's lifestyle despite their retaliations. Many whites believed that the way to solve the indigenous problem was to utilize a certain religion, Christianity, to convert the "savages" and then force them onto reservations—demoralized and decimated.

The railroad spawned many boomtowns that attracted riff-raff and many people from every walk of life—gamblers, gunslingers, pickpockets, prostitutes, preachers, entrepreneurs, outlaws, miners, and the list goes on, to replace the Native Americans and repopulate the coveted land.

On July 24, 1870, the first cross-country train left San Francisco, California, and in a few days arrived in New York City, New York. The feat was heralded by many, which opened the way to even more expansion in the future. Union Pacific chief engineer Grenville Dodge may have put it best when he looked down the track and said: "Gentlemen, *this* is the way to India."

Bibliography

Athearn, Robert G., *American Heritage New Illustrated History of the United States*, Volume 5, *Young America*, Fawcett Publications, Inc., One Astor Plaza, New York, N.Y., 1963.

Coit, Margaret L., *The Life History of the United States*, Volume 3, *The Growing Years*, Time-Life Books, New York, 1963.

Dungan, Myles, *How the Irish Won the West*, Skyhorse Publishing, New York, N.Y., 2011.

Jackson, Rex T., *A Steamy Ozarks Past*, Vol. 2, No. 2, The Ozarks Reader Magazine, Neosho, Missouri, 2005.

Kreck, Dick, *Hell on Wheels: Wicked Towns along the Union Pacific Railroad*, Fulcrum Publishing, Golden, Colorado, 2013.

Legrand, Jacques, *Chronicle of America*, Chronicle Publishing, Inc., Mount Kisco, New York, 1989.

Thorp, Judge Joseph, *Early Days in the West*, Irving Gilmer Publisher, Liberty, Missouri, 1924.

Twain, Mark, *Life on the Mississippi*, American Publishing Company, Hartford, 1883.

Ruff and Romantic Era of the Stagecoach and Pony Express

YOUNG America, before the completion of the transcontinental railroad and the telegraph, depended upon other options to move passengers, freight, and mail to the west coast. The ruff, rugged, dangerous, and romantic period of the stagecoach and Pony Express lasted less than a decade, but was a unique, historic time of westward expansion and national growth.

During the 1800s prior to the American Civil War, a number of stage lines were established to offer western travel and connect the nation. It was a primitive way but faster than the wagon trains that had lumbered and meandered across the Great Plains and over the unforgiving Rocky Mountains. In this way, however, many adventurers headed for the goldfields of Colorado and California to seek fame and fortune—or, possibly, to pursue a new life in the rip-snorting, rip-roaring Wild West as farmers, entrepreneurs, laborers or what-have-you.

On March 3, 1857, the need for speed prompted the United States Congress to pass a bill which would create America's first cross-country mail delivery service. The champions of the bill was Congressman John S. Phelps of Missouri and Senator William M. Gwinn of California. The task of awarding the mail route was given to the postmaster general who selected John Butterfield of Utica, New York, William G. Fargo, and a few other investors for the

$600,000 per year subsidy to carry and delivery the mail in the West.

The Butterfield Overland Mail Stagecoach Route started in St. Louis, Missouri, by way of the railroad to its terminus (end of the line) at Tipton, Mo., where passengers and the United States mail was loaded onto a horse-drawn stagecoach which followed a route coursing south through such Missouri towns and stage stops as Wheatland, Bolivar, Springfield, Ray House, Ashmore, Crouch, Cassville, and Harbin Station; and in Arkansas, from the Elkhorn Tavern to Fort Smith; from there, for example, it went to places like El Paso, Texas, Yuma, Arizona, and through Los Angeles, California, and north to San Francisco. The trip covered about 2,800 bone-jarring miles—a large semicircle across much of America that some dubbed the Oxbow Route.

Along the trail from Tipton to San Francisco about 200 relay (or "swing stations") and "home stations" were utilized and maintained by blacksmiths, wheelwrights, veterinarians, cooks, and others to care for the passengers, coaches, livestock, and whatever was necessary. Butterfield's stage line had hundreds of horses, mules, and coaches to operate the route. The Concord coach, built by Abbot-Downing Company of Concord, New Hampshire, was used, as well as the "celerity" mud wagon which was made in Troy, New York. The stagecoaches were usually pulled by four to six horses or mules, which could travel about 100 miles a day over level terrain. The Butterfield Overland Mail Stagecoach Route ran day and night through and over mountains, arid landscapes, prairies, and hostile Indian lands.

The maiden journey of the Butterfield line began on September 16, 1858, after arriving from St. Louis by rail to Tipton. The stage departed with fanfare—with John Butterfield, the president of the line, and five other passengers including Waterman Ormsby, a news correspondent for the New York *Herald*; the driver of the coach was Butterfield's son. When the stage reached Fort Smith, Arkansas, all the passengers disembarked with the exception of reporter Ormsby, who continued west towards San Francisco—the end of the line.

While all of this was taking place, another Butterfield stage had left San Francisco at the same time heading east. After the

Stagecoach and Pony Express

The Butterfield Overland Mail and Stagecoach Route revisited Cassville, Missouri, for its 150th Anniversary on September 11, 2008.

eastbound arrived at Fort Smith, Butterfield boarded the coach and headed back to Tipton. When the stage rolled into Tipton, Butterfield gathered up the mail from the coach and took the train back to St. Louis to deliver the mail at the post office—the eastbound stage from San Francisco had taken 24 days and 18 hours to make the historic trip. The westbound coach from Tipton took 23 days and 23 hours to reach its terminus and deliver the mail it was carrying; the stage had made Los Angeles on October 7, 1858.

About such arduous overland journeys, Mark Twain who had made the trip himself and wrote about it in his well-known book *Roughing It*, offered a vivid recollection of his experience crossing the Great Plains to Nevada. After purchasing his ticket for $150 at St. Joseph, Missouri (by this time, because of the outbreak of the Civil War, the Butterfield Overland Mail Route had been relocated to a safer northern route), Twain cleverly describes the wide-open prairie that stretched out "for seven hundred miles as level as a floor." He reported taking naps on the top of the coach that flew along at about ten miles per hour. He remembered, as only Twain could, how the sagebrush resembled a "venerable live-oak tree reduced to a little shrub two feet high." The antelope and buffalo peaked his interest and the coyote he explained away as "a long, slim, sick-and-sorry-looking skeleton, with a gray wolfskin stretched over it." His journey took him along the Oregon Trail to the Rocky Mountains, through the famous South Pass, and on through Salt Lake City, Utah, and the alkali desert of Nevada. By the time he had reached his journey's end, however, Twain claimed he had to search diligently through an unabridged dictionary to come up with the right, descriptive words to explain just how thrilled he was to finally reach his destination; he got off the stage at Carson City (named after "Kit" Carson), Nevada—20 days out of St. Joseph, Mo., and the stage continued on without him to Sacramento, California.

The stagecoach drivers were heralded for their long suffering at the reins, enduring Indian attacks, inhospitable weather, threats from highwaymen, and many other things. Mark Twain felt that the "stage driver was a hero [much like how he felt about steamboat pilots]—a great shining dignitary, the world's favorite son, the envy of the people...." It was an honor if the stage driver invited or allowed a passenger to sit down beside him at his work overlooking his team and the trail ahead.

During that era there were many stagecoach lines that sprang up, and one of the other routes that was well-known was the Central Overland California and Pike's Peak Express Company; it was created when the Holladay Overland Mail and Express Company merged with the Overland Dispatch. The Central Overland California and Pike's Peak Express Company ran from Atchison, Kansas, to Placerville, California. The advent of the railroads and the telegraph eventually doomed, for the most part, stagecoach travel.

Another icon of that period in time was the Pony Express. Hundreds of curious spectators turned out on April 13, 1860, in Sacramento, California, to witness the arrival of the first express delivery. In a cloud of trail dust a young Pony Express rider, Tom Hamilton, with a satchel of 49 letters and three newspapers, galloped into town from a history-making 11-day journey which started in St. Joseph, Missouri, at the Pike's Peak Stables. The 1,966 mile ride across the wild and wooly Western frontier was the brainchild of William H. Russell and Alexander Majors of the Central Overland California and Pike's Peak Express Company. With about 500 horses and 119 station stops, excellent Pony Express riders dared and braved the elements and other hairbreadth dangers to deliver important messages and the mail at a breakneck speed. Station stops were positioned at about 25 mile intervals and riders were expected to make 75 miles a day.

American author Mark Twain also bore witness to the Pony Express, and about one of those pony riders he wrote: "He rode a splendid horse that was born for a racer and fed and lodged like a gentleman; kept him at his utmost speed for ten miles, and then, as he came crashing up to the station where stood two men holding a fresh impatient stead, the transfer of rider and mail bag was made in the twinkling of an eye, and away flew the eager pair and were out of sight before the spectator could get hardly the ghost of a look...There were about eighty pony riders in the saddle all the time, night and day, stretching in a long scattering procession from

Missouri to California, forty flying eastward, and forty toward the west."

Although a number of riders may have made a name for themselves, there was one rider for the Pony Express that became a household name: William F. Cody, better known as "Buffalo Bill." Cody was branded with this colorful name because of the time he spent as a buffalo hunter, killing about 4,280 buffaloes in about a year-and-a-half to provide fresh meat to the hungry men building the Union Pacific Railroad; "Wild Bill" Hickok and "Calamity" Jane also rode for the Pony Express and carried the mailbag (or *mochilla*).

In October 1861, the regular Pony Express service was discontinued when the Pacific Telegraph Company had finished their transcontinental telegraph cable across the continent. It helped to end a brief era in American history—the longest stagecoach route in the world and the unique, cross-country mail express of horse and rider. The telegraph and railroad had served to help silence wagon trains, steamboats, stagecoaches, ships, and other early American champions of the West.

Bibliography

Angus, Fern, *Down the Wire Road in the Missouri Ozarks*, Litho Printers, Cassville, Missouri, 1992.

Barnard, Edward S., *Story of the Great American West*, The Reader's Digest Association, Inc., Pleasantville, New York, 1977.

Halleck, Reuben Post, *History of Our Country*, American Book Company, New York, 1923.

Jackson, Ryan J., *Springfield Historic Marker along the Old Butterfield Stage Route*, Vol. 4, No. 1, The Ozarks Reader Magazine, Neosho, Missouri, 2007.

Kreck, Dick, *Hell on Wheels: Wicked Towns along the Union Pacific Railroad*, Fulcrum Publishing, Golden, Colorado, 2013.

Legrand, Jacques, *Chronicle of America*, Chronicle Publications, Inc., Mount Kisco, New York, 1989.

Twain, Mark, *Roughing It*, 1872; (as quoted in *History of Our Country*, Reuben Post Halleck, American Book Company, New York, 1923).

Wexler, Bruce, *How the Wild West was Won*, Skyhorse Publishing, New York, 2013.

"Black Bart": California's Poetic Highwayman

BANKERS, businesses, and prospectors working the goldfields of California's Gold Country, in order to transport the precious cargo, often turned to stagecoaches to do the job. The trails and rugged landscape offered a challenge to the stages when carrying the heavy loads. Unfortunately, however, it wasn't just the terrain and weight of the load that worried most of those involved with the shipments, but thieves, outlaws, and highwaymen. One of the stage lines that had its share of troubles and problems during the Gold Rush era was Wells, Fargo and Company.

The Wells, Fargo and Company was established in 1852 by Henry Wells and William George Fargo. The company's home office was kept in downtown San Francisco, California, at 420 Montgomery Street. The Wells, Fargo and Company eventually merged with the American Express Company, and from 1868 to 1881, Fargo served as the President of the well-known express firm. The company offered financing, gold trading, and express cargo service for such things as gold dust and gold and silver bullion; and just about anything needing to be transported.

The stages, many times traveling through secluded areas suited to the dangers of being held up and robbed, were attacked and confronted on a number of occasions. Desperadoes who cared little for a laborious lifestyle—which, they believed was nothing more

(From: *When a Man's a Man*, Harold Bell Wright, A.L. Burt Company, New York, 1916.)

than a dead-end-street leading nowhere, saw the gold-ridden stagecoaches an easy target that led to the good life. And so, the pesky robbers had to be dealt with, especially the ones that had made a habit of it, like "Black Bart" who was believed to have robbed twenty-eight stages between 1875 and 1883—an average of more than three per year.

The blue-eyed, gray-haired, Charles Earl Bowles, also known as Boles, Bolton, T.Z. Spalding, Po8, and most commonly as the infamous Black Bart, was born in Norfolk, England, in 1829. When Charley was about 2-years-old he moved to America with his parents, John and Maria; and his siblings, and settled in upstate New York on a farm. When Charles was about 20-years-old he decided it was high time to venture out into the world; however, most sources say that he was accompanied by a brother or two. The band of brothers headed for the goldfields in the Wild West, but in 1850 Charles lost his brothers to illness—and, after some soul-searching he headed back east.

On his way home he spent some quality time in Decatur, Illinois, where he met Mary Elizabeth Johnson. A love affair ensued and the two were hitched. The couple had four children, by some accounts, but at the outbreak of the American Civil War in 1861, Charles felt the need to enlist in the Union army. He was mustered into the 116th Illinois Infantry, part of the 15th Army Corps under Major General William Tecumseh Sherman, and the 1st Brigade under Brigadier General Giles A. Smith. Bowles fought and served in 1862 and 1863 in Maj. Gen. Sherman's Yazoo River Expedition in the Mississippi River-Vicksburg area conflicts at Fort Hindman, Jackson, the Siege of Vicksburg, and so on. Bowles went on to fight in Atlanta, Georgia, and in Sherman's March to the Sea. In 1864, however, he was wounded but was able to eventually pull himself together and rejoin his regiment and continue serving until the end of the Civil War in 1865. His time spent in the war probably helped to make Bowles the tough individual that enabled him to do some of the difficult things that lay ahead for him in his California outlaw career.

After returning home to his wife and family, they decided to purchase a small farm in New Oregon, Iowa; but, farm life did not suit the restless heart and spirit of Charles Bowles so he once again answered the call of the wild and meandered to the West, but without his family. He found himself in the Big Sky Country of Montana where he began to work a mining claim where he utilized the available water in the process of panning for gold. By and by he was confronted by the Wells, Fargo and Company with the proposition of buying out his claim, but when he turned down their offer they severed his only water source which forced him to give up his dream of striking it rich; this probably did not sit well with Bowles.

Leaving his Montana mine and shaking the dust from his feet he left the area and headed south to California and put down his roots. Ironically, before long, Wells, Fargo and Company (based in the Bay Area) began to experience a string of robberies. Between 1875 and 1883, a masked, keenly-dressed, polite in behavior, chaste in speech highwayman roamed the trails in order to victimize the stage line—taking the strongbox, rifling the mail, passengers, and stealing anything that was of value.

The Wells, Fargo and Company's Special Officer's Department reporting from San Francisco on November 30, 1888, claimed that the outlaw which had become known as Black Bart was a person of great endurance, a real mountaineer who could traverse hills and ruff terrain with ease; he was well educated and up to date on current events, and cool, calm, and collected.

One unusual thing that set Black Bart apart from other criminals was the fact that he left poems at the scene of many of his crimes. A sampling of his work went like this:

> "Here I lay...down to sleep
> To wait the coming morrow,
> Perhaps success, perhaps defeat
> And everlasting sorrow."

For years the poetic bandit stumped the authorities; he hit Wells Fargo stages time and again on many of their routes, on the Sonorato-Milton, Fort Ross-to-Russian River, Quincy-to-Oroville, Bieber-to-Redding, Downieville-to-Nevada City, Eureka-to-Ukiah, and so on. Black Bart's luck finally ran its course, though, and on account of his last robbery in 1883 he would earn a few years at San Quentin Prison. As the story goes: A firefight broke out during the robbery and while making his get-a-way he dropped a handkerchief which had a laundry mark on it—F.O.X.7. Agents with the Wells, Fargo and Company, James B. Hume and Henry Nicholson Morse, after visiting 91 laundry businesses in-and-around San Francisco, they hit pay-dirt at the American Laundry, which led them to 37 2nd Street where a certain Charles E. Bolton was living—it was Black Bart. In the poetic bandit's hotel room the detectives discovered a half-written letter that matched the handwriting to the poems left behind at the crime scenes. Black Bart was quickly sentenced; however, because of good behavior he was released on January 23, 1888, before he had served his full sentence.

Afterwards, Charles Bowles spent about two weeks in San Francisco while agents kept a close eye on his movements, whereabouts, and activities. After this, he wandered to Modesto, Madera, Merced, and Visalia before disappearing forever.

Possibly wanting to dish out yet one more helping of revenge, a Wells Fargo stage was held up in November 1888 by a masked bandit who matched the description and profile of Black Bart who had left behind his calling card—a poem. Detective Hume, maybe trying to sidestep and avoid embarrassment or incompetence, contended that the robbery of the stagecoach was probably the clever work of a Black Bart copycat. The crime was never solved and never repeated. The truth of what became of the outlaw remains a timeless, unsolved mystery of the American West.

Bibliography

Enss, Chris, *Outlaw Tales of California: True Stories of the Golden State's Most Infamous Crooks, Culprits, and Cutthroats*, TwoDot, Guilford, Connecticut, 2013.

Greene, Francis Vinton, *Campaigns of the Civil War*, Vol. 8, *The Mississippi*, 1882.

McNab, Chris, *Gunfighters: The Outlaws and Their Weapons*, Thunderbay Press, San Diego, California, 2005.

Turner, George, *Gun Fighters*, L. Baxter Lane Publisher, Amarillo, Texas, 1972.

Wexler, Bruce, *How the Wild West was Won*, Skyhorse Publishing, New York, 2013.

Oklahoma Indian Territory: The Final Frontier

THE LAST straw for Indian autonomy began in the late 19th century when Indian Territory (Oklahoma) was opened to white homesteaders. Squeezed and pushed onto reservations and into the Indian Nations, the frontier that Native Americans had enjoyed for thousands of years would vanish; their freedom, independence, and way of life was slipping away before their very eyes. The lands of present-day Oklahoma were promised to them and their children by treaty, and whites were forbidden by law to colonize the territory. In 1879 and 1880, President Rutherford B. Hayes set forth proclamations to stop white settlers from encroaching and intruding into the Nations; however, the law was constantly ignored and the cry for opening up the final frontier for settlement continued to increase in volume.

About the situation, in James Mooney's *Myths of the Cherokee* it reveals how "Thousands of intruders had settled themselves upon the lands of each of the civilized tribes [Creek, Cherokee, Choctaw, Chickasaw, and Seminole], where they remained upon various pretexts in spite of urgent and repeated appeals to the government by the Indians for their removal. Under treaties with the five civilized tribes, the right to decide citizenship or residence claims belonged to the tribes…but the intruders…became so numerous and strong that they had formed an organization…with attorneys and ample funds to defend each claim in outside courts against the decision of the tribe…." The Cherokee and the other civilized tribes

Fort Gibson in Fort Gibson, Oklahoma.

Oklahoma Indian Territory

complained and protested, but without avail.

The "Sooners," (the name given to the whites who had crept into the last remnant of the old Indian Territory before it was opened to settlers) were, for the most part, made up of deputies, land surveyors, and railroad workers who had the advantage of knowing the region beforehand; others, known as "Moonshiners," preferred to sneak in by moonlight past the Federal troops who were stationed there to keep order and prevent such things.

On April 22, 1889, by proclamation of President Benjamin Harrison, Indian Territory was opened to homesteading. About 200,000 land-grabbing souls had amassed in southern Kansas and northern Texas along the borders of the once-protected Oklahoma District waiting for the signal to be given to start the greatest, frenzied land rush in American history. At noon, to the echoing sound of gunfire, a wild stampede of ruff and tough "Boomers" swarmed and flooded across the coveted border on horseback, in buggies, wagons, prairie schooners, on foot, bicycle, and by any means to stake their land-claims. For justification, the region had been dubbed by the media as the "last barrier of savagery" left in America.

Besides homesteads, tent towns blossomed almost overnight, like Oklahoma City and Guthrie, which went on to become the first capital of the new state. It was only the beginning, other portions of Indian Territory, such as the Cherokee Strip, was eventually ratified by Congress to be opened to the public for settlement. On September 16, 1893, a pistol shot signaled over 100,000 homesteaders to run and compete for 40,000 claims; the mad dash, however, caused the death of a few of the participants when they were killed in the stampede of humanity.

Concerning the cession of the Cherokee Strip, Mooney wrote: "It was known to the Cherokees that for some time would-be settlers on the lands of the outlet had been encamped in the southern end of Kansas, and by every influence at their command had been urging the Government to open the country to settlement and to negotiate with the Cherokees afterwards, and that a bill for that purpose had been introduced in Congress."

From 1876 to 1900, Colorado, Montana, North Dakota, South

Dakota, Washington, Idaho, Wyoming, and Utah, joined the Union and became states. On November 16, 1907, Oklahoma became the forty-sixth state of the United States; the last states to join the Union in the continental United States was Arizona and New Mexico in 1912.

Native Americans had ruled themselves, more or less, until the Indian Intercourse Act of 1834. A land boom, orchestrated mostly by a greedy bunch of railroad executives and real estate agents—to pressure the government to snatch the region which 75,000 Indians called home, was too much of a selfish temptation to ignore. Indian Territory had become Oklahoma, "without the formal consent of [its] inhabitants," but this time around there was no forced removal, the whites had no other place to put American Indians. The clever phrase-machine of John Lewis O'Sullivan's "Manifest Destiny," had finally worked its magic to conclusion and the continental Untied States was complete with the addition of Arizona and New Mexico—the West had finally been taken and tamed.

Bibliography

Legrand, Jacques, *Chronicle of America*, Chronicle Publications, Inc., Mount Kisco, New York, 1989.

Mooney, James, *Myths of the Cherokee*, Nineteenth Annual Report of the Bureau of American Ethnology to the Secretary of the Smithsonian Institution, 1900.

Muzzey, David Saville, *The United States of America: II From the Civil War*, Ginn and Company, Boston, 1924.

Roark, James L., *The American Promise: A History of the United States*, Bedford Books, Boston, 1998.

Wexler, Bruce, *How the Wild West was Won*, Skyhorse Publishing, New York, 2013.

Jim Bridger:
Solving Western Mysteries

BEFORE AND AFTER Meriwether Lewis and William Clark brought back their reports of the glorious Western realities, many outlandish beliefs were entertained in the imagination of the American people. Some maintained that prehistoric woolly mammoths were still wandering and roaming the unknown region; the reports of Yellowstone's geysers, hot springs and boiling mudholes was thought by some to be wild, fictitious tales; and some believed that the West contained a mountain of rock salt that measured about 45 by 80 miles in size; still others considered the possibility of the existence of erotic dwarfs or the devil's "Inferno." The rumors abounded for a number of years while daring and brave mountaineers, fur trappers, and explorers continued to prove them wrong with their reports and discoveries of the frontier.

As the stories of "Colter's Hell" and "Bridger's Lies" slowly subsided, St. Louis, Missouri, became famous for the beaver furs that flooded in from the West. In this lucrative environment, businessmen like John Jacob Astor, who was the great-grandfather of the Astor who perished in a watery grave aboard the ill-fated *RMS Titanic* on April 15, 1912, made a fortune during the beaver-pelt era and passed it on to his heirs. Overtime, the public's opinion and preposterous notions that first circulated faded into history, replaced by the continued stories of disasters, Indian attacks, and golden opportunities.

TIMELESS STORIES OF THE WEST

About the life and times of the Western mountain men and explorers, Francis Parkman, author of *The Oregon Trail: Sketches of Prairie and Rocky-Mountain Life*, wrote that they would "lounge about the fort, or encamp with his friends in its vicinity, hunting, or enjoying all the luxury of inaction; but when once in pursuit of the beaver, he was involved in extreme privations and perils. Hand and foot, eye and ear must be always alert. Frequently he must content himself with devouring his evening meal uncooked, lest the light of his fire should attract the eyes of some wandering Indian; and sometimes, having made his rude repast, he must leave his fire still blazing, and withdraw to a distance under cover of the darkness, that his disappointed enemy, drawn thither by the light, may find his victim gone, and be unable to trace his footsteps in the gloom."

It must pay to advertise—when William Henry Ashley posted his famous "want" ad in the Missouri *Gazette and Public Advertiser* on February 13, 1822, soliciting young men to join him in his scout corps venture, a number responded and went on to become celebrated, iconic American trailblazers, like Jedediah Strong Smith, Tom Fitzpatrick, Hugh Glass, William and Milton Sublette, James Clyman and Edward Rose. Another one in Ashley's "Westering" party was James ("Jim") Bridger, who went on to become one of America's most unsung trader, explorer, and scout.

James Bridger was born March 17, 1804, in Richmond, Virginia, and worked as an apprentice to a blacksmith until he relocated to St. Louis, Missouri. After joining Ashley's group, he began his long journey of becoming one of the most accomplished and important figures of the American West.

In 1823 as they were approaching an Arikara Indian village near what is now the border of North and South Dakota, they were suddenly attacked and overwhelmed by about 600 warriors armed with muskets, bows and arrows, and tomahawks; Bridger's group had about 70 men in the foray. It didn't go well—about 12 were killed during their hasty retreat.

A year later, while in the confluence area of the Green and Bear Rivers in Utah, Bridger followed the Bear River to where it emptied into a large, shallow bay; after he had tasted the salty water he was inclined to conclude that it must be part of the Pacific Ocean, when

Jim Bridger

Author's illustration of a mountain man.

in fact it was the Great Salt Lake. Up to this time, the saltwater lake had only been seen by Native Americans.

For about twenty years Bridger lived the adventurous life of a grizzled trapper and meandered about the region from Canada to southern Colorado and from the western Missouri River country to Idaho and Utah. From 1832 to 1835 he served as a guide for a number of expeditions in the West under Benjamin Louis Eulalie de Bonneville, an American army captain who later attained the rank of general.

Bridger's next significant contribution to the settlement of the West was the establishment of Fort Bridger in southwestern Wyoming for overland pioneers traveling the Oregon Trail. Fort Bridger was built in 1843 in the river bottoms of Black Fork near the site of present-day Fort Bridger, Wyoming. The fort offered supplies for wagon trains headed to Oregon and California; however, within about three years much of their traffic chose the northern "Greenwood Cut-Off"—favoring its more direct route. During one season, Bridger acted as a guide for trophy-hunting Sir St. George Gore of County Sligo, Ireland, to hunt for bear and bison to add to his collection. (Sligo is located in the northern part of Ireland where the Garavogue River enters Sligo Bay from Lough Gill.) A modern-day sign was eventually placed in Colorado which read: "Gore Pass, Altitude 9,000 feet: Here in 1855 crossed Sir St. George Gore, an Irish baronet bent on slaughter of game and guided by Jim Bridger. For three years he scoured Colorado, Montana, and Wyoming, accompanied usually by forty men, many carts, wagons, hounds, and unexampled camp luxuries. More than 2,000 buffalo, 1,600 deer and elk, and 100 bears were massacred for sport." Bridger's association with the fort ended in 1855 when he sold out to the Mormons, as many of them were migrating to the West.

By this time the progress in the region had tempted many other daring individuals to make the journey-effort. St. Louis was bubbling over with activity related to the movement, and according to Francis Parkman: "Not only were emigrants from every part of the country preparing for the journey to Oregon and California, but an unusual number of traders were making ready their wagons and outfits for Santa Fe. The hotels were crowded, and the gunsmiths

Jim Bridger

and saddlers were kept constantly at work in providing arms and equipments for the different parties of travelers. Steamboats were leaving the levee and passing up the Missouri crowded with passengers on their way to the frontier."

Like the many caravans headed West, Bridger's career was ongoing as well, and in 1856 he discovered "Bridger's Pass" in central Wyoming. In 1859 and 1860 he trekked into Yellowstone and after seeing its natural wonders, he couldn't help but spread the good news about it which came to be known as Jim Bridger's Lies. The myths and legends surrounding Yellowstone, however, lingered for about another decade before all the colorful reports were finally confirmed.

One of the regions most famous spectacles is "Old Faithful," one of 200 geysers which erupts at intervals of 37 to 93 minutes and shoots as high as 170-feet into the air. There are more than 3,000 geysers and hot springs in the area. The region became the Yellowstone National Park on March 1, 1872; it covers an area of 2,221,772.61 acres, mostly in the northwest corner of Wyoming. The Yellowstone area was first visited by John Colter around 1807.

Eventually, at this time, Bridger retired to a farm located near present-day Kansas City, Missouri, but was sought out by the United States government for a number of special assignments; serving as a guide and scout for General Albert S. Johnson in Utah; helping to measure the distance of the Bozeman Trail from Fort Kearney, Nebraska, to Virginia City, Montana; and in 1865 he showed General Greenville M. Dodge's surveying crew how to get the Union Pacific Railway through the rugged Western mountains.

Concerning the mountain man era and its earlier glory of unknown mysteries and beauty, Francis Parkman reminisced on September 16, 1892: "He who feared neither bear, Indian, nor devil, the all-daring and all-enduring trapper, belongs to the past, or lives in a few gray-bearded survivals. In his stead we have the cowboy, and even his star begins to wane."

In 1868, in his "twilight" of life, Jim Bridger retired to a farmstead in Santa Fe, Missouri—and, reportedly, took to the enjoyment of books. He died quietly at his farm on July 17, 1881, while his rugged and wondrous Western mysteries were well on their way to being completely solved. Engraved on his tombstone were these words:

"We miss thee in the circle around the fireside,
We miss [you] in devotion at peaceful eventide,
The memory of your nature, so full of truth and love,
Shall lead our thoughts to seek [you] among the blest above."

Jim Bridger

Bibliography

Athearn, Robert G., *American Heritage New Illustrated History of The United States*, Vol. 6, *The Frontier*, Fawcett Publications, Inc., One Astor Plaza, New York, N.Y., 1963.

Chronicle of America, Chronicle Publications, Mount Kisco, New York, 1989.

Funk & Wagnall New Encyclopedia, Funk & Wagnall, Inc., New York, 1979.

Gilbert, Bil, *The Old West: The Trailblazers*, Time-Life Books, Alexandria, Virginia, 1973.

Harris, Bill, *How the West was Won: The Mountain Men*, Skyhorse Publishing, New York, N.Y., 2011.

Parkman, Francis, *The Oregon Trail: Sketches of Prairie and Rocky-Mountain Life*, Boston, Little Brown, and Company, 1892.

Parrish, William E.; Jones, Jr., Charles T.; Christensen, Lawrence O., *Missouri: The Heart of the Nation*, Forum Press, Inc., Arlington Heights, Illinois, 1980.

Additional Illustrations

A Butterfield Overland Mail Stagecoach revisiting Cassville, Missouri, for its 150th Anniversary on September 11, 2008.

Typical log construction was utilized by many early American pioneers.

The beaver was prized by fur trappers and traders.
(From: *Little Journeys to Alaska and Canada*, Marian M. George,
A. Flanagan Company, Chicago, 1901.)

Above: Fort Osage National Historic Landmark on the Missouri River just north of Buckner, Missouri; founded on September 2, 1808, and served until 1822. Below: One of the reproduced buildings in Fort Osage.

Inside the "Factory House" at the Fort Osage National Historic Landmark near Buckner, Mo.

Illustration of a grizzly bear.
(From: *Little Journeys to Alaska and Canada*, Marian M. George,
A. Flanagan Company, Chicago, 1901.)

"Nathan Boone Home" at the Nathan Boone Homestead State Historic Site located just north of Ash Grove, Missouri; built in 1837 of hand-hewn ash logs.

Gravestone of Nathan Boone at the Nathan Boone Homestead State Historic Site near Ash Grove, Mo.; notice the Nathan Boone Home in the background.

Inside the Nathan Boone Home; one of the home's fireplaces can be seen through an interior doorway.

Ashmore Station Memorial Stone and Marker just south of Springfield, Missouri, on the Butterfield Overland Mail Route (1858-1861).

Crouch Station Memorial Stone on the Butterfield Overland Mail Stagecoach Route just north of Cassville, Missouri (1858-1861).

The American Bison.

A 21st century diesel-electric train.

Illustration of an early American trapper.
(From: *History of Our Country*, Reuben Post Halleck, American Book Company, New York, 1923.)

The "Ray House" at the Wilson's Creek National Battlefield near Springfield, Missouri, which served as a stage stop for the Butterfield Overland Mail.

The "Elkhorn Tavern" at the Pea Ridge National Battlefield near Pea Ridge, Arkansas, which served as a stage stop for the Butterfield Overland Mail.

A dogtrot-style log cabin at the Fort Gibson Historic Site in Fort Gibson, Oklahoma.

Index

Index

A

Adams, John Quincy, 67
Allen, Paul, 21
Arbuckle, Matthew, 93
Arthur, Chester A., 33
Ash Grove, Missouri, 93, 94, 95
Ashley, William Henry, 31, 33, 35, 124
Astor, John Jacob, 123
Atchison, Kansas, 107
Atkinson, Henry, Gen., x
Atlanta, Georgia, 98

B

"Baby Doe," Tabor, 12, 13, 14
Bad Axe River (Wisconsin), x, xi
Bainbridge, New York, 31
Bartleson, John, 73
Bates County, Missouri, 20
Bent, Charles, 79
Benteen, F.W., 46
Benton, Thomas Hart, 33
Bent's Fort, 79, 80
Bent, William, 79
Biddle, Nicholas, 21
Bidwell, John, 73
Big Foot (Chief), 60
Bismarck, North Dakota, 45
Black Fish (Chief), 27, 29
Black Hawk (Chief), x, xi, 10
Black Kettle (Chief), 87, 88
Blow, Henry, 33
Boone, Daniel, 23, 25, 26, 27, 28, 29, 91, 92
Boone, Daniel Morgan, 92
Boone, James, 27
Boone, Moses, 95
Boone, Nathan, 92, 93, 94, 95
Boone, Preston, 95
Boston, Massachusetts, 2
Boudinot, Elias, 40
Bowles, Charles Earl ("Black Bart"), 113, 114, 115
Bozeman Trail, x
Braddock, Edward, 25, 29
Brannan, Samuel, 74
Bryan, Rebecca, 25, 28
Bridger, Jim, 123, 124, 127
Buchanan, Elizabeth, 33
Buchanan, James, 33
Butler, Missouri, 18
Butterfield, John, 103, 104

C

California Gold Rush, 2
California *Star*, 74
Campbell, Robert, 33
Cape Horn, South America, 2, 97
Carson, Christopher ("Kit"), 80, 106
Cashman, Fanny, 3, 7
Cashman, Nellie, 1, 2, 3, 4, 5, 7
Cassiar District, British Columbia, 3
Cassville, Missouri, 105
Central City, Colorado, 13
Charleston, South Carolina, 98
Cherokee Phoenix, 40
Cherry Creek, Colorado, 9

153

Index

Chihuahua, Mexico, 20
Chivington, John M., 10, 87
Chouteau, Auguste, 49, 51
Clanton, Billy, 4
Claremore, Oklahoma, 38
Clark, George Rogers, 65
Clark, William, ix, 17, 21, 31, 33, 52, 53, 54, 55, 67, 123
Cobh, Ireland, 2
Cody, William F., 108
Coloma, California, 2, 74
Colter, John, 52, 53, 54, 55, 123, 127
Cool, William, 26
County Armagh, Ireland, 13
County Cork, Ireland, 1, 2, 7
County Tyrone, Ireland, 33
Crazy Horse (Chief), 46, 47
Cripple Creek, Colorado, 13
Cunningham, Thomas J., 3
Custer, George Armstrong, 45, 46, 47, 60, 87, 88

D

Dawes, Henry L., 57
Dawson City, Alaska, 5
Decatur, Illinois, 113
Defiance, Missouri, 28, 91
Democratic Review, 1, 68
Denver, Colorado, 9, 12
Dickson, Joseph, 52
Dodge, Grenville Mellen, x, 100, 101, 127
Dodge, Henry, 92
Dubuque, Julien, 19

E

Eads, James Buchanan, 33, 95
Earp, Wyatt, 4
Emory, William H., 80
Eureka Springs, Arkansas, 99

F

Fairbanks, Alaska, 7
Fargo, William G., 103, 111
Finley, John, 26
Fitzpatrick, Tom, 80, 124
Forsyth, James, 61
Fort Abraham Lincoln, 45
Fort Bellefontaine, 19
Fort Bennett, 60
Fort Bridger, 126
Fort Cobb, 87
Fort Dodge, Kansas, x
Fort Gibson, 93, 118
Fort Laramie, Wyoming, 79
Fort Lyons, 10
Fort Ross, 73
Fort Smith, Arkansas, 104, 106
Fort Supply, 87
Fremont, John Charles, 20, 73, 80

G

George, Marian M., 32
Glass, Hugh, 124
Gould, Emerson, 33
Grant, Ulysses S., 2, 33
Grove, Oklahoma, 24

Index

Guthrie, Oklahoma, 119
Gwinn, William M., 103

H

Halleck, Reuben Post, 44
Hamilton, Alexander, 88
Hamilton, Lewis M., 88
Hancock, Forrest, 52
Harris, Benjamin, 33, 119
Hawken, Samuel, 33
Harrodsburg, Kentucky, 65
Hawks, Francis, 27
Hayes, Rutherford B., 117
Hearst, George, 45
Hazen, W.B., 87
Hickok, "Wild Bill," 108
Holden, Joseph, 26
Holiday, "Doc," 4
Hook, George, 12
Hotchkiss, Benjamin Berkeley, 61
Howard, Benjamin, 92
Hume, James B., 115

I

Irish Land League, 4

J

Jackson, Helen H., 57
Jackson Hole, Wyoming, 33
Jackson, Seth Nathan, 11, 81
Jefferson, Thomas, ix, 17, 67
Johnson, Mary Elizabeth, 113

K

Kandern, Baden, Germany, 71
Kansas City, Missouri, 127
Kearny, Stephen Watts, 80
Keogh, Myles, 47

L

Laclede, Pierre, 49, 51
La Junta, Colorado, 79
Leadville, Colorado, 12
Lewis, Meriwether, ix, 17, 21, 31, 52, 53, 54, 55, 67, 123
Little Falls, Minnesota, 19
Lisa, Manuel, 52
Longisland, North Carolina, 26
Los Angeles, California, 34
Low Dog, 46

M

"Manifest Destiny," 10, 43, 68, 69, 120
Manuel, Fred, 45
Manuel, Moses, 45
Marshal, James Wilson, 2, 74, 76
Marthasville, Missouri, 28
McCourt, Elizabeth Bonduel, 12
McDougall, T.M., 46
McGillycuddy, Vallentine, 59, 60
McKinley, William, 33
McLaughlin, James, 60
McLowry, Frank, 4

Index

McLowry, Tom, 4
Merrick, George Byron, 50
Miles, Nelson A., 60
Mission Santa Gertrudis, 5
Monay, James, 26
Mooney, James, 37, 117
Morse, Henry M., 115
Murrieta, Joaquin, ii, 75, 76
Muzzey, David S., 66

N

Natchitoches, Louisiana, 20
New Helvetia, California, 73
New Haven, Missouri, 54, 55
New York *Herald*, 104
New York City, New York, 101
Norman, Ruth, 14
Northwest Territory, Alaska, 6

O

Oklahoma City, Oklahoma, 119
Oshkosh, Wisconsin, 12
O'Sullivan, John L., ix, 1, 67, 68, 120

P

Papinville, Missouri, 18, 20
Parkman, Francis, 124
Pierce, Franklin, 68
Pike, Zebulon Montgomery, 17, 18, 19, 20, 21
Phelps, John S., 103
Placerville, California, 107
Potts, John, 53

Price, Sterling, 33
Promontory Point, Utah, 100
Pueblo, Colorado, 20

Q

Queenstown, Ireland, 2

R

Rapid City, South Dakota, 60
Reading Pennsylvania, 23, 29
Red Cloud (Chief), 45
Reno, M.A., 46
Richmond, Virginia, 124
Rische, August, 12
RMS Titanic, 123
Rogers, Will, 38
Roosevelt, Theodore, 33
Ross, John, 40
Routt, John L., 9
Russell, William H., 107

S

Sacramento, California, 2, 100, 107
Sallisaw, Oklahoma, 40
Sand Creek Massacre (Colorado), x, 10
San Diego, California, 35
San Francisco, California, 2, 3, 7, 72, 101, 104, 106, 111, 114, 115
Sans Oreille (Chief), 20
Santa Fe, New Mexico, 20, 34
Santa Fe Trail, x, 21, 34, 35, 80

Index

Schiefflin, Ed, 4
Sequoya, 37, 38, 39, 40, 41
Sheridan, Philip Henry, x, 45, 87
Sherman, William Tecumseh, 87, 113
Sitting Bull (Chief), 46, 47, 60
Skagway, Alaska, 5
Smith, Jedediah Strong, ix, 31, 33, 34, 35, 124
Sonora, Mexico, 75
South Pass, x
Steward, John, 26
St. Louis, Missouri, 17, 19, 28, 29, 31, 33, 35, 49, 51, 52, 55, 73, 91, 104, 106, 123, 126
St. Vrain, Ceran, 80
Sublette, William, ix, 33, 34, 124
Sutter, John Augustus, 2, 71, 73
Sutter's Mill, ix, 71

T

Tabor, Augusta, 12
Tabor, Elizabeth Lillie, 14
Tabor, Horace Austin Warner, 12, 13
Tabor, Rose ("Silver Dollar"), 14
Tahlequah, Oklahoma, 86
Taos, New Mexico, 79
Tipton, Missouri, 104
Tombstone, Arizona, 4
Trenton, New Jersey, 17
Tucson, Arizona, 4
Tuskegee, Tennessee, 37

Twain, Mark, 49, 51, 53, 92, 95, 106, 107

U

United States Magazine, 1, 68
Utica, New York, 103

V

Victoria, British Columbia, 3, 7

W

Washington, George, 88
Washita Massacre (Oklahoma), x, 87, 89
Wells, Henry, 111
Wheat Ridge, Colorado, 14
Whiteside, General, x
Wilkinson, James, 19
Wilson, Jack, 58
Wilson, Woodrow, 33
Womack, Bob, 13
Wounded Knee Massacre (South Dakota), x, 47, 60
Wovoka, 58, 59, 61

XYZ

Other Books by Rex T. Jackson

The Sultana Saga: The Titanic of the Mississippi
James B. Eads: The Civil War Ironclads and His Mississippi
A Trail of Tears: The American Indian in the Civil War
Traces of Ozarks Past: Outlaws, Icons, and Memorable Events
Monumental Tales from the Ozarks
Notable Persons and Places in Missouri's History

About the Author

Rex T. Jackson's work has appeared in a number of publications, like **The Ozarks Mountaineer**, **Blue and Gray**, **Good Old Days**, **Ancient American**, **Capper's Weekly**, **Back Home**, **The Ozarks Reader**, **Route 66 Magazine** and others. He became a staff member of **The Ozarks Mountaineer** (based in the Branson, Missouri area) for several years and eventually founded **The Ozarks Reader Regional Magazine** and served as publisher and editor from 2004 through 2012.

www.ingramcontent.com/pod-product-compliance
Lightning Source LLC
Chambersburg PA
CBHW050815160426
43192CB00010B/1764